LIFE IN
ANCIENT ROME

LIFE IN
ANCIENT ROME

Art and literature, religion and mythology, sport and games, science and technology:
the fascinating social history of emperors, senators, citizens, slaves and the people of Rome

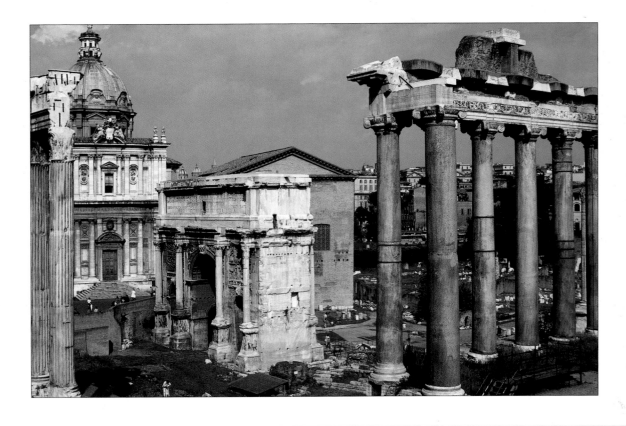

How the Romans lived their daily lives, at work and at home, lavishly illustrated
with more than 250 superb paintings, drawings, photographs, maps and plans

NIGEL RODGERS

CONSULTANT: DR HAZEL DODGE FSA

southwater

This edition is published by Southwater, an imprint of
Anness Publishing Ltd, Hermes House, 88–89 Blackfriars Road,
London SE1 8HA; tel. 020 7401 2077; fax 020 7633 9499

www.southwaterbooks.com; www.annesspublishing.com

Anness Publishing has a new picture agency outlet for images for
publishing, promotions or advertising. Please visit our website
www.practicalpictures.com for more information.

UK agent: The Manning Partnership Ltd;
tel. 01225 478444; fax 01225 478440
sales@manning-partnership.co.uk
UK distributor: Grantham Book Services Ltd;
tel. 01476 541080; fax 01476 541061; orders@gbs.tbs-ltd.co.uk
North American agent/distributor: National Book Network;
tel. 301 459 3366; fax 301 429 5746; www.nbnbooks.com
Australian agent/distributor: Pan Macmillan Australia;
tel. 1300 135 113; fax 1300 135 103
customer.service@macmillan.com.au
New Zealand agent/distributor: David Bateman Ltd;
tel. (09) 415 7664; fax (09) 415 8892

Ethical Trading Policy

At Anness Publishing we believe that business should be conducted in an
ethical and ecologically sustainable way, with respect for the environment
and a proper regard to the replacement of the natural resources we employ.

As a publisher, we use a lot of wood pulp to make high-quality paper for
printing, and that wood commonly comes from spruce trees. We are
therefore currently growing more than 500,000 trees in two Scottish forest
plantations near Aberdeen – Berrymoss (130 hectares/320 acres) and West
Touxhill (125 hectares/305 acres). The forests we manage contain twice
the number of trees employed each year in paper-making for our books.

Because of this ongoing ecological investment programme, you, as our
customer, can have the pleasure and reassurance of knowing that a tree is
being cultivated on your behalf to naturally replace the materials used to
make the book you are holding.

Our forestry programme is run in accordance with the UK Woodland
Assurance Scheme (UKWAS) and will be certified by the internationally
recognized Forest Stewardship Council (FSC). The FSC is a non-
government organization dedicated to promoting responsible management
of the world's forests. Certification ensures forests are managed in an
environmentally sustainable and socially responsible basis. For further
information about this scheme, go to www.annesspublishing.com/trees

Publisher: Joanna Lorenz
Senior Managing Editor: Conor Kilgallon
Editors: Joy Wotton and Elizabeth Woodland
Designer: Nigel Partridge
Cover Designer: Nigel Partridge
Illustrations and maps: Vanessa Card, Peter Bull Art Studio
Production Manager: Steve Lang

© Anness Publishing Ltd 2007

A CIP catalogue record for this book is available from the British Library.

Previously published as part of a larger volume, *The Roman World*

Front cover, clockwise from top left *scene wall of the Theatre Sabratha;
Sabratha, Antoine Temple; Leptis Magna, market stall; Temple of Apollo,
Pompeii; Sabratha, a mosaic with temple of the Isis in the distance;
plan of Rome showing the imperial metropolis at its prime; Interior of the
Colosseum; Virgil (70-19BC) and the Muses, from Sousse (Hadrumetum)
(mosaic) Roman, (3rd century AD); House of Dancing Faun, Pompeii;
Arches of the Colosseum; Theatrical masks on the retaining wall of the
Theatre of Sabratha; Map of the Roman Empire; The Colosseum, rooms
and passage ways beneath the arena floor;* **front cover flap** *The Pantheon,
Rome;* **back cover flap** *Map of the Roman Empire and its neighbours
AD212;* **page 1** *The Colosseum;* **page 2** *The Arch of Severus, Forum
Romanum;* **page 3** *Forum Romanum;* **page 4** *Preserved ancient water
supply in Pompeii;* **page 5 (top)** *Temple of Antoninus and Faustina, Forum
Romanum;* **page 5 (bottom)** *Hadrian's Wall, England.*

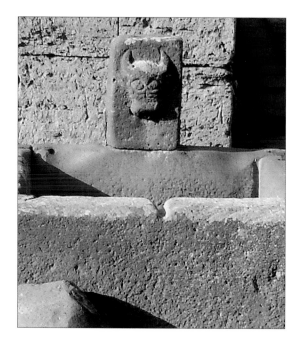

Acknowledgements

Art Archive: 106t /Galleria Borghese Rome/Dagli Orti 60–1, 31b, 39b,
52b, 59b, 67b, 85b, 86t, 101b, 108b, 109t, 110t, 116t, 118tr, 123t, 124t,
/Bardo Mus. Tunis/Dagli Orti 47t, 49t, 72tr, 89t, 108t, 111t, 115t, /Santa
Costanza Rome/Dagli Orti 127b, /Archaeological Mus. Madrid/ Dagli Orti
68b, /Bibliothèque des Arts Décoratifs Paris/Dagli Orti 82b, 107t, /Museo
della Civita Romana Rome/Dagli Orti 56b, 68t, 70t, 73tr, 85t, 89b, 90t,
100t, 102t, 103t, 104b, 111b, 122t, 126t and b, /Museo Capitolino
Rome/Dagli Orti 54t, 58t, 125b, 127t, /Archaeological Mus.
Naples/Dagli Orti 13t, 23b, 55t and b, 63t, 71t, 97t, 98t, 99t, 102b, 112t,
113t, 119t, 121t, 121b, 122b, 124t, /Archaeological Museum Istanbul/Dagli
Orti 118bl, 120t, /Archaeological Mus. Sousse Tunisia/Dagli Orti 11t,
/Musée du Louvre Paris/Dagli Orti 14t, 54t, 62t, 73b, 95b, 96t, 103b,
120b, /Museo Nazionale Terme Rome/Dagli Orti 16t, 40t, 66b, 69b, 97b,
121t, /Biblioteca Nazionale Marciana Venice/Dagli Orti 19t, /Provinciaal
Mus. G M Kam Nijmegen Netherlands / Dagli Orti 24b, /Archaeological
Mus. Florence/ Dagli Orti 28b, /Cathedral Treasury Aachen/Dagli Orti 32t,
/Villa of the Mysteries Pompeii/ Dagli Orti 42–3, 52t, /National Mus.
Damascus Syria/ Dagli Orti 44l, /Musée Granet Aix-en-Provence /Dagli Orti
44br, /Cathedral Mus. Ferrara/ Dagli Orti 49b, /Archaeological Mus.
Ostia/ Dagli Orti 53b, 84b, 88, 109b, /Museo Nazionale Romano Rome
57b, /Museo Opitergino Oderzo Treviso /Dagli Orti 62b, /Archaeological
Mus. Sfax/Dagli Orti 66t, /Archaeological Mus. Merida/ Spain/ Dagli Orti
67t, /Musée de la Civilisation Gallo-Romaine Lyons /Dagli Orti 69t,
/National Archaeological Mus. Athens/ Dagli Orti 72b, /Archaeological
Mus. Alexandria/Dagli Orti 80t, /Museo Concordiese Portogruaro/Dagli
Orti 84t, /Musée d'Orsay Paris/Dagli Orti 86b, /Museo Nazionale
Ravenna/Dagli Orti 91b, /Musée des Antiquités St Germain en
Laye/ Dagli Orti 92t, 114b, /Archaeological Mus. Cherchel Algeria/Dagli
Orti 92b, 93t, /Musée de Cluny Paris/Dagli Orti 119b.
Bridgeman Art Library: 8–9, 11b, 13b, 14t, 18tl, 21b, 23t, 33b, 51b.
Corbis: 38b, /Araldo de Luca 17, 18b, 24tl, 25t, 28t, 29b, 35t, 37tl and br,
41t and b, 45br, 50, 56t, 71b, 99b, 106b, 115b, /Mimmo Jodice 10t, 15t,
24tr, 26–7, 31t, 32b, 46t and b, 48t and b, 70b, 90b, 113b, /Michael S.
Yamashita 22t, /Sandro Vannini 29t, 76t, 100b, /Alinari Archives 36b, 63b,
64t, /Archivo Iconografico, S.A. 34b, 64b, 65b, 107t, 110b, 117t, /David
Lees 16b, /Michael Nicholson 81t, /John Heseltine 77b, /Roger Wood
12b, 20t, 53t, 65t, 105t, 123b, /Vanni Archive 10b, 22b, 117b, /Tony
Brown/Ruggero Vanni 30b, /Bettmann 101t, /Massimo Listri 15b, 34t,
/Werner Forman 30t, 35b, 38t, 125t, /Stapleton Collection 79t, /25b,
/Chris Hellier 20b, /Philip Spruyt 21t, /Dave Bartruff 36t, /Gérard
Degeorge 39t, /Origlia Franco/Corbis Sygma 45t, /Charles and Josette
Lenars 47b, 59t, /Elio Ciol 58b, /Christel Gerstenberg 74–5, /Enzo and
Paolo Ragazzini 79b, /Roger Antrobus 80b, /Franz-Marc Frei 94–5, /X.
Noticias 104t.
Mary Evans Picture Library/Edwin Wallace: 82t
Photo Scala, Florence: /© 1990 40b, 51t, 87, 116b, /courtesy of the
Ministero Beni e Att. Culturali 19b, 33t, 76b, /© 2003/Fotografica
Foglia 78, /© 1998 98b.

CONTENTS

INTRODUCTION

For centuries, Rome eclipsed all other cities. Its vast population, enriched by the taxes and tribute of the empire, sucked in raw materials, goods and human beings, many of them slaves, both from around the Mediterranean and from farther afield. In order to supply Rome, traders explored new routes across the known world, bringing exotic goods back to the city. Fleets of huge ships set sail annually from Egypt, Spain and Africa with vital cargoes of grain and olive oil to feed the city, while agents roamed the empire to find wild beasts whose violent deaths would amuse the Roman populace.

The urban life that developed in Rome after 150BC anticipated some aspects of modern city life, with its tall blocks of apartments, mass entertainments, high crime rates and problems with water supply and sewage disposal. However, Rome also offered opportunities that attracted free men to settle there, with its theatres, temples, libraries and lecture rooms and popular entertainments such as the arena or the baths.

Despite numerous artworks adorning the city – it was joked Rome had more statues than living inhabitants – Roman culture was predominantly literate. A knowledge of both Greek and Latin was essential for any aspiring educated man. Women too could often read and, although barred from public life, played a greater role in Rome than in some other cultures. All these splendours were made possible by slavery, but slavery took many forms and lacked any hint of a colour bar. This allowed freed slaves to become citizens and to rise in what was, in some ways, a meritocratic civilization.

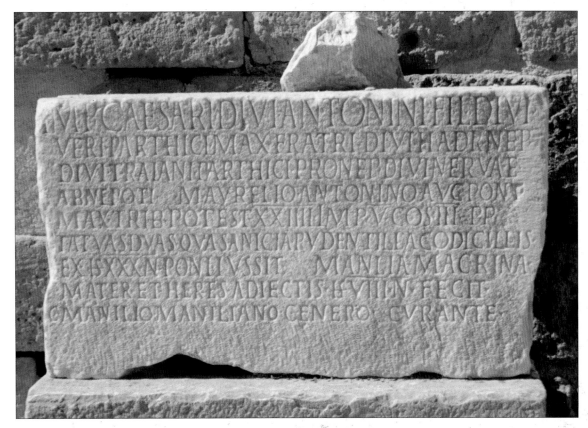

Opposite: Looking west into the interior of the Colosseum. This amphitheatre had seating for 50,000 spectators. Below the arena floor was a complex set of rooms and passage ways for wild beasts and other provisions.

Right: An inscription from Sabratha, now in modern Libya, home of one of the best-preserved of all Roman amphitheatres.

LITERATURE

The story of Latin literature begins with two great comic playwrights, Plautus and Terence, and the epic poet Ennius *c.* 200BC. Latin as a language survived the end of the West Roman empire in AD476 and continued to be used up to the 1960s by the Catholic church, which in the early Middle Ages had had a near monopoly on literacy. Latin remained the language of much science and diplomacy until the late 17th century in western Europe – Isaac Newton, a Protestant Englishman, wrote most of his scientific works in Latin.

Considered of central importance in education into the mid-20th century, Latin is still admired for its clarity and brevity and is useful for medicine, natural science and law. Ignoring the fall of Rome, poets carried on writing in Latin through the Middle Ages, and the language enjoyed a classicizing revival during the Renaissance (1400–1600) in western countries.

The great pioneers of Latin literature, especially the writers of its golden age (*c.* 70BC–AD14), were conscious of their debt to Greek literature, with seven brilliant centuries of achievement behind it. Ultimately the Greeks inspired rather than crushed their Roman followers. Roman poets such as Virgil, Horace and Ovid and prose writers such as Cicero created a classical style comparable to that of Greek writers. For the Roman empire was an empire of letters as well as of arms; literacy being relatively widespread. Sadly much Latin literature has perished, hand-copied books and scrolls being few and fragile.

Left: View of Tivoli with Rome in the distance, painted by Gaspard Poussin in the 17th century. Tivoli was a favourite retreat of writers and emperors such as Horace and Hadrian.

THE FIRST ROMAN WRITERS

Above: A portrait of Menander, the Athenian comedian who so influenced Roman playwrights.

Below: The theatre at Pompeii, built in the 2nd century BC, long before Rome had a permanent theatre. Its original plan followed Greek models in having a narrow stage front, but it was later remodelled by the Romans.

Latin literature got off to a flying start with Plautus, a comic genius who knew how to entertain still relatively simple Romans with hilarious slapstick comedies. Terence wrote less rumbustiously and with less success for a possibly more select audience. Enough survives to give us a good idea of both their works, but only fragments remain of the work of their great contemporary, Rome's first epic poet, Ennius. All three adapted Greek originals for Roman audiences.

PLAUTUS *c.* 254–184BC

Born to poor parents in Umbria, Plautus worked as a stage carpenter among other jobs and only started to write plays in middle age. He then became Rome's most successful adapter of Greek "new comedy". (This was derived from the work of the Athenian Menander, who had lived 100 years before, and of other Greeks whose works have been lost.) Plautus reputedly wrote 130 plays, of which 21 survive. Written in verse, like Greek comedies, they usually involve characters with Greek names in Greek cities. However, Plautus was mainly concerned with getting laughs from his audience, so he sacrificed consistency or subtlety of character for jokes and puns, far easier to accomplish in Latin than Greek.

Plautus often replaced spoken dialogue with songs accompanied by pipe music or with *cantica*, duets or solo arias, producing what might be called Roman comic opera or musical comedy. The result was an earthier, cruder comedy than that of Menander, and proved immensely popular and influential. Shakespeare and Molière, the French 17th-century playwright, were indebted to him in their plays such as *The Comedy of Errors* or *L'Avare*, while comic opera, pantomime and television sitcoms today are Plautus' distant but direct heirs.

Performed at first in makeshift wooden theatres, his comedies were, like the Greeks', usually linked with religious festivals, but as time went by they came to be seen as entertainment. In a typical early play *Aulularia* (*The Pot of Gold*), Euclio, a poor elderly Athenian, discovers a hoard of gold and becomes obsessively suspicious of his daughter's suitor, who he fears is after it. All ends happily, however, after various alarms. In *Captivi* (*The Prisoners*) an old Greek, Hegio, buys prisoners of war, hoping to exchange one for his captured son. Two such prisoners, master and slave, secretly swap identities. The master is freed to negotiate the return of Hegio's son and the slave is finally revealed as Hegio's other son, kidnapped in childhood. In one of Plautus' most famous plays, *Bacchides* (*The Bacchis Sisters*), a dishonest slave called Chrysalus (Goldfinger) dominates the action, scheming to defraud his master, as he proudly tells the audience. Confusion is increased by two prostitutes who are both called Bacchis. Cunning slaves, desperate young lovers and miserly, jealous old men are among Plautus' stock characters.

TERENCE *c.* 195–159BC
Born in North Africa and brought to Rome as a slave, Terence (Publius Terentius Afer) gained his education, his freedom and his entrée to aristocratic circles through his talents and good looks. Closer to the Greek model than Plautus', Terence's plays are concerned with love affairs and complications arising from ignorance or misunderstandings. Only one play, *Eunuchus* (*The Eunuch*) enjoyed popular success, because he added broad comedy to it. Normally, Terence retained the original Greek irony, translating Attic (Athenian) Greek into elegant, pure Latin that lacked Plautus' verbal exuberance. The resulting plays, six of which survive, found little favour with still unsophisticated Roman audiences but became part of the classical canon. Terence bitterly attacked the gladiators, tight-rope walkers and others who proved more popular than his plays but was himself criticized by literary men for cannibalizing different Greek plays to make his own. Although he died young during a visit to Greece, his influence on later European comedy of manners was huge.

ENNIUS 239–169BC
Called the father of Latin poetry, Ennius was actually born to a Greek family in Calabria. (Southern Italy was then known as Magna Graecia, greater Greece, being deeply Hellenized.) After serving with the Roman army in Sardinia, Ennius came to Rome with Cato the Elder *c.* 204BC and ultimately gained Roman citizenship.

Ennius began writing epic poetry late in life, dying impoverished but confident of posthumous fame, as he claimed to be a reincarnation of Homer, the great Greek poet. Unfortunately, only fragments of his work survive, but they reveal his versatility, for he wrote tragedies, comedies, satires and other works. His greatest work was his *Annals*, a poetic history of Rome from Aeneas' flight from Troy to his own day. The work extended to 20,000 lines, written in the smooth-flowing Homeric hexameter (a verse line of six metrical feet) he introduced from Greek.

Ennius' few surviving lines, which are quoted by later writers such as Virgil, mingle high Greek heroism with Roman alliteration and love of puns. Although later sometimes mocked for clumsiness, Ennius was the first to show that Latin poetry could achieve epic greatness by adopting Greek classical forms.

Above: Scene from a comedy by Plautus, the first and always the most popular Roman playwright. His fame spread around the empire, as this 3rd century AD mosaic from Sousse in Africa shows.

Below: A portrait of Ennius, the first Roman epic poet who came to see himself as a reincarnation of Homer. Ennius also wrote tragedies and comedies for the stage.

AUGUSTUS' POETS LAUREATE

Above: Scene from the Prima Porta statue showing Augustus' diplomatic victory in 19BC when Parthia returned Roman legionary standards, a victory which Horace duly praised as effective poet laureate.

Below: A mosaic shows the poet Virgil writing The Aeneid *between the muses Clio (history) and Melpomene (tragedy). Virgil's epic became popular across the empire.*

Although neither Virgil nor Horace sought the role, both became, in effect, poets laureate for Augustus. Although very different – Virgil introspective, moody, Horace urbane, if keenly aware of life's sorrows and joys – both wrote supremely classical verse.

VIRGIL 70–19BC

Perhaps the greatest of all Roman poets, Virgil (Publius Vergilius Maro) was born near Mantua, in Cisalpine Gaul, which was by then almost fully Roman. His parents were only modest farmers, but Virgi was well educated and became closely involved in imperial affairs. He lived through civil wars that wrecked the Republic – there were wars in 16 of the 51 years of his life – and lost his farm in the chaos following the Battle of Philippi.

However, it was returned to him after an appeal to Octavian and he died rich, leaving 10 million sesterces. Such experiences deepened the longing for peace which permeates his poetry.

Virgil's first work, *The Eclogues*, written before 37BC, is set in an idealized Arcadia, influenced by Theocritus (310–250BC). It depicts shepherds' lives and loves but also refers to recent troubles, such as farmers' arbitrary evictions. *Eclogue IV* contains a passage in which the Sybil, Rome's oracle, foretells the birth of a divine child who will restore the golden age. *Jam redit et virgo, redeunt Saturnia regna…*("Now the Virgin returns, the reign of Saturn returns …"). Actually praising the Julian family, this was interpreted by Christians as a prediction of the birth of Christ.

Virgil was now given substantial properties by Maecenas, who acted as patron for many poets under Augustus. His next work, *The Georgics*, appeared in 29BC. Its praise of Italian farm life – echoing Hesiod's *Work and Days* of *c.* 700BC – marvellously evokes the beauties of the Italian landscape but is of limited use as a farming manual. Pressed to write an epic about the emperor, Virgil instead responded with *The Aeneid*.

This work relates the legendary adventures of Aeneas, the Trojan prince who fled burning Troy to found Lavinium, Rome's legendary precursor. As the Julians claimed descent from Aeneas, this was subtle flattery. Aeneas is no bloodthirsty hero but an upright man who hates – yet excels at – fighting. His betrayal of Dido, queen of Carthage, appears shabby but he is driven by his destiny to abandon her. (Dido despairingly kills herself.) Virgil, who died before he completed his epic, wanted it destroyed, but after Augustus published it, it became accepted as Virgil's masterpiece, vital to Rome's self-image.

While rivalling Homer's *Iliad* in scope and grandeur, the *Aeneid* takes no delight in war. Instead it stresses Rome's responsibilities as ruler. *Hae tibi erunt artes, pacisque imponere morem/ Parcere subjectis et debellare superbos* ("These shall be your skills: to impose peace, spare the conquered and overthrow the mighty").

The epic starts majestically:

Arma virumque cano, Trojae qui primus abo oris

"Arms and the man I sing, who, forced by fate
And haughty Juno's unrelenting fate
Expelled and exiled, left the shore.
Long labours both by sea and land he bore."

> (translated by John Dryden)

HORACE 65–8BC

The son of a freedman (ex-slave) who had prospered enough to pay for his education in Athens, Horace (Quintus Horatius Flaccus) fought on the wrong Republican side at the Battle of Philippi in 42BC. Returning unhurt but penniless to Italy, he was introduced to Maecenas' circle by Virgil *c.* 37BC, later becoming a sincere supporter of the Augustan settlement. Maecenas gave him a small farm in the Sabine Hills at Tivoli near Rome. There Horace built a villa which he celebrated in his poems, but he was also a sociable man of the world.

Horace's *Satires* (*c.* 35BC) contain little satire in today's sense but praise Maecenas, a friend as well as patron, and include a tribute to his father, in lively, colloquial Latin. Celebrating peace after Actium (31BC), Horace produced the *Epodes* (lyric poems). Inspired by Archilochus (*c.* 640BC), they deal mostly with love and politics but also praise rural life: *Beatus ille, qui procul negotiis...* ("Happy the man who far from business, ploughs again his ancestral lands").

The poor reception for his first book of *Odes* in 23BC upset him, but they contain his finest poetry. They celebrate the return of spring: *Diffugere nives: redeunt jam gramina campis/Arboribusque comae...*

("The snows have fled. The grass returns already to the meadows, and leaves to the trees"); the joys of drinking: *Nunc est bibendum* ("Now's the time to drink!") and the passing of youth: *Ehue fugace, Postume, Postume/Labuntur anni, nec pietas moram...*("Alas, Postumus, Postumus, the years slide swiftly away and piety will not fend off wrinkles, old age or death..."). He ends triumphantly, proclaiming artistic immortality: *Exegi monumentum aere perennius* ("I have created a work longer-lasting than bronze...").

Horace had no successor as poet laureate, but some poems speak as freshly today as ever: *Dum loquimur, fugeret invida/Aetas: carpe diem, quam minimum credula postero.* ("While we talk, hateful time runs on. Seize the fruits of today, never rely on the future."

Above: A mural from Pompeii showing a wounded Aeneas being tended by a doctor.

Below: Virgil reading The Aeneid *to Augustus, as painted by Ingres, c. 1812.*

CATULLUS AND THE ELEGIAC POETS

Above: The Venus de Milo, one of the most famous portrayals of the goddess of love in antiquity. Venus was a deity of overwhelming importance to the elegiac poets, whose poems deal primarily with affairs of the heart and of lust.

Below: Catullus, the supreme Latin poet of love, fancifully depicted reading a poem, in a painting by Stepan Bakalovich in 1885. In reality, Catullus was passionate but hardly romantic like this.

The last decades of the Republic and first years of the Empire (Principate) saw huge political and social changes in Roman life that inspired the *Neoterici* (New Poets) to experiment radically. Greek models gave Catullus, then Propertius and Tibullus, the means by which to create new, more direct and moving forms of Latin poetry. (The description of these poets' work as Elegiac refers to their hexameter/pentameter metre. It does not mean that they wrote funereally!)

CATULLUS 84–54BC

Born at Verona, Catullus (Gaius Valerius Catullus) was a leader of the *Neoterici*, or New Poets. His father was rich enough to entertain Julius Caesar but Catullus had no interest in politics. He owned a villa on Lake Garda, whose beauties he praised, but spent most of his short life in Rome and most of his energies on literature and love. In Rome he fell in love with Clodia, called Lesbia in his poems, who was probably the sister of Clodius Pulcher – Cicero's enemy – and Catullus'

social superior. Lesbia/Clodia became his obsession, adored then reviled in 25 brilliant, brief poems. For poetic models Catullus looked back to polished Alexandrians such as Callimachus (*c.* 320–240BC) and to Sappho (*c.* 600BC), perhaps the greatest woman poet, who wrote on love's bitter-sweet joys and torments. Catullus' poetry, mingling passion, urbanity and awareness of life's transience, raised colloquial Latin to new heights.

Amemus mea Lesbia atque vivemus /Rumoresque senum severiorum. "Let us live and love my Lesbia, and ignore all old men's censorious talk", begins one poem addressed to her, which continues, "We, when our brief day is done, must sleep in everlasting night". He goes on to urge her in vivid, demotic Latin, *Da mi basia mille, deinde centum /Dein mille altera, dein secunda centum.* "Give me a thousand kisses, then a hundred, then another thousand and a second hundred".

Unlike most Greek poets, Catullus was writing about an individual woman at a time when aristocratic women in Rome were enjoying novel freedom and could appreciate – or reject – such admiration. Clodia seems to have rejected him, so Catullus later wrote angrily, *Odi et amo*, "I hate and I love" and described Lesbia "Giving herself to the sons of Remus", (becoming a common prostitute).

Catullus could also write in other ways. He lyrically mocked Lesbia's dead sparrow, for example: *Lugete, o Veneres Cupidenesque…* "Mourn, you Venuses and Cupids, and all men of true feeling. My lady's sparrow is dead". He also savagely lampooned his contemporaries.

Although what won Catullus contemporary renown were long mythological poems such as *Peleus and Thetis*, he was indisputably one the world's greatest lyric love poets.

PROPERTIUS *c.* 54–16BC

Son of an equestrian (knight) of Perugia, Propertius (Sextus Propertius) probably had a legal training in Rome as a young man. In Rome he became friends with Virgil and Ovid and then with Maecenas, who gave him a house on the fashionable Equiline Hill. Propertius, however, had little interest in political life and refused Maecenas' request to write an epic about Augustus. Instead, his poems concentrate on his love life, especially his relationship with Cynthia.

Cynthia seems to have been either a high-class courtesan or a widow of independent mind and wealth. She used both to torment Propertius – or so his poems imply, depicting him in a grovelling role that was novelly demeaning for a Roman knight. His first book of poems was dedicated to, and about, Cynthia. *Non ego nunc tristes vereor mea Cynthia, Manes/Nec moro extremo debita fata rogo* … "I don't fear death's sad kingdom, Cynthia, nor resent being doomed to the funeral pyre at the last, as I have a fear that is harder than death itself – that I may no longer be loved by you when I die". Propertius' affair with Cynthia started in *c.* 30BC and lasted about five years, during which time his passion cooled as Cynthia was often unfaithful to him. For solace from love's torment Propertius turned not to nature – he was very metropolitan – but to art. He talked knowledgeably about classical Greek painters such as Apelles and some of his poems apparently describe scenes from extant wall-paintings.

TIBULLUS *c.* 50–19BC

Handsome and wealthy, the son of an equestrian, Tibullus (Albius Tibullus) differed from Propertius in his love for the countryside. His first poems describe an idyllic existence far from city cares. However, Tibullus resembled Propertius in that he too was in thrall to a mistress. Delia – another pseudonym – had little time for such bucolic joys and clearly had the upper hand in their relationship. Her

successor in Tibullus' affection was the even more demanding and ominously named Nemesis. Tibullus also fell in love with a boy, Marathus, who spurned him but used him to help pursue a girl. Tibullus dwells masochistically on his suffering in this love triangle. It is uncertain how much of the three extant books in Tibullus' name is really his own poetry.

MAECENAS THE PATRON

The greatest literary patron of the Roman empire under Augustus, Maecenas claimed descent from Etruscan kings. One of the young Octavian's key ministers, he was renowned for discovering promising poets. Virgil and Horace were protégés who repaid his support with great poetry praising the new regime. Maecenas himself reputedly had luxurious, even decadent tastes, as surviving fragments of his own poetry suggest, affronting Augustus' official restoration of Roman *virtus*. Maecenas lost official favour well before his death in 8BC, but his name lives on as the archetypal patron.

Above: The Surrender of Briseis, *from the House of the Tragic Poet at Pompeii. Briseis was a slave girl in* The Iliad *who Achilles, bitterly jealous, had to hand over to Agamemnon. Catullus wrote on the subject with typical bitter-sweet passion.*

Below: A view of Lake Garda in northern Italy, Catullus' birthplace, whose beauties he was the first to praise.

OVID AND LATER SILVER AGE POETS

Above: An amber figurine of Cupid and Psyche from the 1st century AD. *Ovid's poetry delighted in such myths.*

Below: Ovid's grandest and most celebrated work, the Metamorphoses, *had a huge impact on later artists and writers. This grand depiction of the myth of Cupid and Psyche was painted by the Renaissance artist Raphael (or his studio) in 1518–19.*

With Ovid, Latin poetry finally attained an elegance, lyricism and wit to rival that of any Greek. His unfading popularity down the ages is partly due to these characteristics, partly to his fantastical invention and partly to his sophisticated eroticism – the last finally led to banishment by Augustus. After Ovid, there was a hiatus in Latin poetry, then two poets of the "silver age" emerged, who attempted with mixed success to emulate the poets of the golden age.

OVID 43BC–*c.* AD18

Born to an equestrian Italian family, Ovid (Publius Ovidius Naso) finished his education with the customary grand tour of Greece before settling in Rome. His first book of poems was the very successful *Amores* (*Loves*). He began writing the first book of the first edition *c.* 25BC, publishing the other four books over the next decade. (The surviving edition dates from *c.* 3BC.)

In his early books Ovid parodied the elegiac poets' love sickness but soon Ovid himself emerged as a fervent if light-hearted lover. Addressed to Corinna – who, unlike the lovers of earlier poets, was probably not an actual mistress, but a composite figure – the *Amores* depict amorous adventures among the more openly frivolous Roman upper classes. In the *Amores*, as in subsequent works, Ovid used myths not for deep psychological resonance but decoratively, to describe a woman's legs for example. If Horace tended to treat love as a light-hearted game from which the poet remains wisely detached, Ovid treated love as the only game worth playing. The title of Ovid's *Ars Amatoria* (*The Art of Love*) mimicks Horace's *Ars Poetica*.

Ovid's longest and most lastingly famous work was the *Metamorphoses*, 15 books of mythology which are epic in scale and by turn bewitching, moving, erotic or witty. At the other end of the scale from Virgil's solemn myth-making, its underlying theme – that everything changes form – included serious comments among its erotica, such as *Video meliora, proboque;/Detrioria sequor* ("I see the better way and approve it, but follow the worse") and *Tempus edax rerum* ("Time, the devourer of all things").

OVID'S EXILE AND DEATH

While many Romans laughed with Ovid, one important Roman was not amused: the ageing emperor. Always annoyed by upper-class promiscuity, Augustus particularly disliked his grand-daughter Julia's behaviour, exiling her for immorality suddenly in AD8. Ovid, caught up in the scandal, was exiled to Tomis on the Black Sea, a cold, unciv-ilized, remote area, now in Bulgaria, then Rome's Siberia. Augustus and his successor Tiberius stonily ignored the poet's piteous pleas to be allowed to return, and Ovid died in exile among a people he found barbarous.

In his last decade Ovid wrote *Tristia* (*Melancholia*) and *Epistulae ex Ponto* (*Black Sea Letters*). The lonely tedium of exile is conveyed by lines such as *Gutta cavat lapidem, consumitur anulus usu* ("Dripping water hollows out a stone, a ring is worn away by use"). However, his fame suffered no eclipse. He was revered throughout the Middle Ages and a bowdlerized version of his works called *Ovid Moralisé* (*Ovid the Moralist*) was circulated widely. The first great poet in English, Geoffrey Chaucer (1340–1400) wrote of "Venus' clerk, Ovid, that hath sown wonder-wide the great god of Love's name". Ovid's fame continued to grow during the Renaissance and after, with many translations or adaptations especially of the *Metamorphoses*.

SILVER AGE POETS

After Ovid's death no significant poet emerged for 40 years until Lucan (Marcus Annaeus Lucan; AD39–65). Born in Spain, a nephew of the philosopher Seneca, Lucan was studying Stoic philosophy in Athens when Nero called him to Rome in AD60. For a short while he enjoyed imperial favour, being made a *quaestor* (magistrate), before he became involved in the Piso conspiracy of aristocrats with Republican sentiments against the despotic emperor. It cost him his life.

Lucan's great work was his uncom-pleted epic *Pharsalia*, which deals with Rome's civil wars of the 1st century BC. He begins with an address to his fellow citizens, not the usual invocation of the Muse: *Quis furor, o cives, quae tanta licen-tia ferri?* ("What was this madness, citizens, this great orgy of slaughter?"). The epic lacks a hero – Julius Caesar is portrayed as villainous and his rival Pompey is not wholly admirable either. Instead it focuses on the internecine bloodshed that wrecked the Republic. Lucan's poem abounds in epigrams, paradoxes and biting wit, with over 100 grand speeches. However, it can be argued that his characters are over-simplifed, his style is sometimes monotonous and that at times Lucan's work degenerates into sentimentality.

Statius (Publius Papinius Statius; AD45–96) was an epic poet who also felt driven to emulate Virgil. His chief work, his *Thebaid*, took him a decade to write. Published in AD92, it dealt with the same Greek legends about Oedipus' curse on Thebes and its traumatic conse-quences that the Athenian dramatist Aeschylus had written about 500 years before. Statius' style is too highly polished and suggests that, like Lucan, he had talent rather than genius. Such legendary heroics were increasingly seen as dated anyway.

Below: Apollo and Daphne, sculpted by Bernini in 1622. The beautiful myth of the transformation of Daphne into a myrtle was wittily retold by Ovid in his Metamorphoses.

GREAT PROSE WRITERS

Rome was a nation of orators schooled in the art of high rhetoric. To match this, Roman writers created prose of unsurpassed power, clarity, pithiness and at times majesty. While there were cogent earlier writers such as Cato the Elder (234–149BC), only in the 1st century BC did Latin prose began to achieve its full, formal splendours, as befitted the language of the new rulers of the world.

CICERO 106–43BC

Marcus Tullius Cicero, statesman and lawyer, wrote on many subjects from astronomy to art and education and in so doing almost invented philosophy in Latin. Caesar, Cicero's political opponent and not modest about his own feats, said that Cicero's was "A greater achievement, expanding the boundaries of Rome's culture, than those of its empire".

Much of Cicero's work, including 900 letters, has survived. This is unusual but hardly accidental: it survived because it was admired and copied. To the critic Quintilian (AD30–c. 100) Cicero was "The name not of a man but of eloquence itself". Cicero's philosophy also deeply affected Augustine, the Christian writer.

Cicero made some of the most brilliant political and legal speeches in Roman history, such as that against Verres, the corrupt ex-governor of Sicily in 70BC, which drove Verres into exile. However, his career as a writer really flowered later during his enforced absence from politics when Caesar dominated Rome (49–44BC). Starting with two minor works of political philosophy *De republica* and *De legibus* (*On the State* and *On the Laws*), he went on to produce *The Paradoxes of the Stoics*, a rhetorical masterpiece in which he argued both sides of a debate (he had studied in Athens under the Sceptics). In 45BC Cicero outlined a plan to "give my fellow citizens a guide to the noblest form of learning" (philosophy). He wrote twelve books over the next two years most – following Plato – in the form of dialogues covering the main schools of ancient philosophy. *De finibus* (*Concerning Ends*) is typical of his brilliant summary of earlier Greek thinkers, notably the Stoics, and is expressed eloquently and clearly in Latin.

Cicero seldom propounded fixed philosophical viewpoints, nor did he claim to be original in his thinking. Instead, however, he established the rendering of basic Greek philosophical terms into Latin – terms such as *qualitas, moralis, beatitudo* for "quality, moral, happiness" – that remain in use today.

In *Scipio's Dream*, Cicero also outlined current geocentric views on the nature of the universe. His letters reveal more about urbane, cultured upper-class Roman life in the late Republic than any others and are profoundly admired even today for their style and humanity.

Above: Marcus Tullius Cicero, the great orator, lawyer, statesman and man of letters. Although seldom an original thinker, Cicero translated major works of Greek philosophy into Latin, summarizing their arguments brilliantly. His superbly readable Letters *inspired generations with their humane and liberal outlook.*

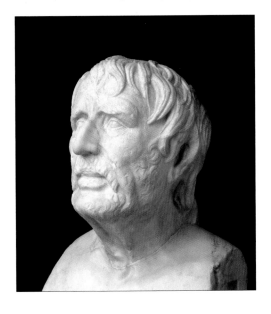

Right: Bust of Seneca, Roman statesman, playwright and philosopher. He was Nero's tutor and adviser before being forced to kill himself.

SENECA 4BC–AD65

A Stoic philosopher, tutor and then minister to the young Nero, a successful if at times unscrupulous businessman, Seneca (Lucius Annaeus Seneca) was also a noted essayist and Rome's greatest tragic playwright.

Seneca's nine plays all deal with Greek legends and have titles such as *Oedipus*, *Hercules* and *Medea*. They are "closet tragedies", intended to be read aloud at small, aristocratic gatherings rather than performed in large Roman theatres.

Although Seneca's dramas hardly bear comparison with their prototypes in classical Athens, they proved very influential later, inspiring Shakespeare and other Renaissance dramatists. His *Epistulae Morales* (*Moral Letters*), 124 brief sermons in letter form dealing with subjects from vegetarianism to the humane treatment of slaves, were equally influential. He also wrote longer essays such as *De clementia* (*On Mercy*).

Seneca was eventually forced to kill himself by Nero after he had been implicated in the Piso conspiracy to assassinate the emperor.

PLINY THE ELDER AD23–79

Pliny (Gaius Plinius Secundus) was a successful Roman administrator of the equestrian order as well as a writer of a boundless, indeed reckless, curiosity that finally killed him. Although he also wrote a history of the German wars, the work which has survived is his *Natural History*. This consists of 37 volumes that represent an encyclopaedia of Graeco-Roman knowledge of the universe, humanity, animals, trees, birds and plants, while also covering in detail medicine and the arts. Edward Gibbon later described it as "An immense register of the discoveries, the arts and the errors of mankind", for Pliny sometimes seems credulous to modern eyes. As commander of the fleet at Misenum near Naples during Vesuvius' eruption in AD79, he tried without success to investigate it and to organize relief efforts but was probably asphyxiated on shore by volcanic gases.

PLINY THE YOUNGER AD61–c. 112

The studious nephew of the elder Pliny who wisely stayed behind at Misenum while his uncle sailed off with the fleet, Pliny the Younger (Gaius Plinius Caecilius Secundus) was tutored by Quintilian.

Pliny had a successful senatorial career, and he finally became a consul under Trajan in AD100. He thanked the emperor for this in his *Panegyricus*, which reveals a talent for fulsome flattery. Far livelier are his letters, many of them written for publication, which give a vivid picture of their age from a cultured noble's viewpoint. His letters to Trajan, written when he was the conscientious if somewhat flustered governor of Bithynia (in north Asia Minor) are also revealing. They cover topics from local fire brigades to the proper way to treat alarming new sects such as the Christians. Pliny the Younger probably died in office.

Above: Using mud to cure skin complaints, as recommended by Pliny the Elder, in a book of 1481.

Below: The oldest extant manuscript of Pliny the Younger's Letters, *dating from the early 6th century* AD.

NOVELISTS AND SATIRISTS

Right: The dreamlike, lyrical quality of Apuleius' The Golden Ass *is echoed in this mosaic from Asia Minor of the 3rd century* AD. *It illustrates the myth of Cupid and Psyche, which forms the core of the book.*

Below: Martial had the whole Flavian dynasty as his patrons, including an unlikely patron in the dour and despotic emperor Domitian (below), chiefly because he only attacked men who had prospered under Nero.

After the heroic age of Roman literature, writers turned increasingly to satire in prose or verse – Juvenal's biting wit effectively created satire in its modern sense – or to novels that were satirical, romantic or both. However, prose fiction was considered a very low literary form.

PETRONIUS (d. AD66)

One of Latin literature's most colourful figures, Petronius (Gaius Petronius Arbiter) was a Roman aristocrat about whom little is known. According to Tacitus, writing decades later, "His days were passed in sleep, his nights in the business and pleasures of life. The reputation that most men win through energy he gained through sloth. Yet as governor of Bithynia and later as consul, he showed himself highly competent". One of Nero's courtiers, Petronius was implicated in the Piso conspiracy and committed suicide – but not before he had recorded all Nero's vices and sent off the list and smashed a precious vase he knew the emperor wanted. His one surviving book – unmentioned by the historian – is his *Satyricon*, a sprawling picaresque novel about some insatiably bisexual adventurers, devoid of morals if not of intelligence, who wander around the Greek cities of southern Italy. They all have Greek names – Encolpion the cultured but depraved narrator, his faithless boyfriend Giton, Ascyltos his rival – following Roman theatrical custom. The most remarkable figure is that of Trimalchio, the multimillionaire freedman (ex-slave) whose gross vulgarity dominates many passages. Petronius was better at catching "street Latin", everyday language, than any writer since Plautus. He records but does not judge – not even the clause of Trimalchio's will which stipulates that all his legatees eat a bit of his corpse before they can inherit. The novel, of which only Books XV and XVI survive, was long considered obscene.

APULEIUS (b. *c.* AD127)

Born in North Africa and educated at Carthage and Athens, Apuleius (Lucius Apuleius) lectured and travelled extensively. He also wrote the only Latin novel to survive complete, *The Golden Ass*. This relates in eleven books the amorous and comic incidents which lead Lucius, a sorcerer's apprentice, to be transformed into a donkey. The rest of the work recounts his varied adventures and misadventures in this form until his final restoration to human shape by the goddess Isis. The longest of these episodes, which takes up about a fifth of the book, is the tale of Cupid (Greek Eros) and Psyche. Parts of this tale, and even more the closing section's vision of Isis, are described with a true religious intensity which is unusually revealing of the depth of pagan devotion to the gods, especially in such an essentially light-hearted work. Although Apuleius may have derived his tale from the Greek poet Lucian's *Metamorphoses*, he wrote a strange, poetic, beautiful and original form of Latin.

MARTIAL (AD40–*c.* 104)
Probably the greatest master of the epigram – a short, sometimes very short, poem with a sting in its tail – Martial (Marcus Valerius Martialis) was born in Spain but spent most of his adult life in Rome. Some 1,500 of his poems survive. Probably helped by his compatriot Seneca at first, he came to know people close to the emperor Domitian, in whose reign (AD81–96) he enjoyed his greatest success. Martial can be human, even genial when writing about children or pets, although at other times his work is blatantly porno-graphic. An early poem, *Liber Spectaculorum* of AD81, celebrated the opening of the Colosseum but he got into his stride with the *Xenia* and *Aphoreta*, which were written between the mid-80s AD and AD97, when he retired to Spain. Martial's dismissive two-liner "On a Critic" is typically pithy: *Versiculos in me narratur scribere Cinna/Non scribit, cuius carmina nemo legit.* ("Cinna is said to write versicles against me. A man whose poems nobody reads cannot be called a writer.")

JUVENAL (*c.* AD60–*c.* 130)
The greatest Roman satirist and the first poet to devote himself to satire in our sense, Juvenal (Decimus Junius Juvenalis) came from a well-off family and held local

Left: Manuscript from the 15th century with a page of Juvenal's satires. The first great poet who can be considered wholly satirical, Juvenal's devastating honesty proved inspirational to later Western satirists.

magistracies. He then fell foul of the emperor Domitian and may have been banished to Egypt before returning to a life of embittered poverty in Rome. His situation improved later under Hadrian and he ended his life in modest comfort, with a small country estate as well as his Roman residence.

Juvenal's early experiences helped shape the jaundiced view he gives of Roman life in which *probitas laudatur et alget* ("Honesty is praised and starves"). His 16 *Satires* were published in 5 books between AD110 and 130. In the first he declared his *saeva indignatio* (fierce indignation) at Roman corruption and vulgarity, but his prudent intention was to attack mainly those who had flourished under Domitian. He lambasted the aristocracy's bad habits – venality, parsimony, sexual voracity – in his first book. *Satire VI* contains a 700-line-long diatribe against women. Markedly misogynistic, it attacks female vanity and virtue. Later satires attack life in the megalopolis more generally: *duas tantum res anxius optat/panem et circuses* ("The populace longs for just two things: bread and circus games").

Below: Juvenal savaged women for wearing too much jewellery in a way that could be markedly misogynistic, so setting an unfortunate example for some later satirists. This mummy portrait of a woman is from Egypt, c. AD120.

LATE ROMAN WRITERS

Above: The Moselle, whose vineyards and slopes Ausonius praised in his longest and most famous poem, Mosella.

Below: St Augustine grew up in the still-thriving province of Africa, whose splendid town life is revealed by these extensive 3rd-century mosaics from Carthage.

The decline of the empire did not see the end of Latin literature, which continued even after Rome's final political collapse in AD476.

AUSONIUS (*c.* AD310–95)

A native of Bordeaux, at whose university he both studied and lectured, Ausonius (Decimus Magnus Ausonius) was a prolific if uneven poet. A summons to the imperial court at Trier to be tutor to the young emperor Gratian led to his meteoric rise: he became governor of Gaul, then Africa and in AD379 consul. After Gratian's murder in AD383, he returned to his native Bordeaux. Letters to his friend St Paulinus of Nola reveal the widening gap between pagans and Christians – Ausonius was basically a pagan. Ausonius' most famous poem, which is lyrical if unoriginal, sings the praise of the beauties of the Moselle valley that he had seen around Trier.

PERVIGILIUM VENERIS (*c.* AD350)

Both the author and date of this beautiful poem are unknown. The title means "Venus' Vigil" and the poem celebrates in 93 haunting, romantic lines the eve of the spring festival of Venus in rural Sicily; the upsurge of new life in flowers, animals and humanity. It has as its refrain *Cras amet quis nunquam amavit...*("Tomorrow let them love who have never loved; and let those who have loved love tomorrow. Spring is new, spring full of song, the springtime of the world is reborn.") Its language forms a link between classical and medieval Latin, while its content makes it a swansong of paganism.

ST AUGUSTINE (AD354–430)

One of the great Church fathers, whose writings are fundamental to both Protestantism and Catholicism, Augustine is also an important figure in both literature and philosophy.

Born in Tagaste, North Africa, his mother was a devout Christian but his father only a reluctant convert. The young Augustine, tormented by sexual urges yet drawn to philosophy, joined the Manicheans, who believed the whole physical world was ruled by the devil. Augustine began teaching in Carthage in AD371 and had a 12-year-long relationship with a woman who bore his son. He only returned to Christianity in AD385 after his move to Rome and a mystical experience in a garden when he heard the voice of God. Intellectually he was influenced both by the teachings of Ambrose, Archbishop of Milan, and by Plotinus, the Neoplatonist whose pagan mysticism Augustine fused with Christianity.

Augustine now began writing the books that make him among the most eloquent of theologians: *Against the Academics, On the Greatness of the Soul, On Free Will* and *Against Faustus the Manichean.* In AD396

Right: The Wheel of Fortune shown in this 15th-century manuscript was one of Boethius' main ideas, inspired by life and death.

he became bishop of Hippo, an African city. He preached to the local people in lively demotic Latin, while writing a more formal classical Latin for his literary peers. His *Confessions*, his literary masterpiece of *c.* AD400, shows an honest, even agonized self-scrutiny unmatched until the 18th century. "Oh Lord make me chaste but not yet!" is its most famous line.

Augustine aggressively propounded orthodox Catholic beliefs against heretics such as the Donatists – who believed that only sinless priests should serve Mass – and Pelagius, a Romano-Briton who believed in human perfectibility. In *On Grace and Free Will*, he argued that every human was damned to hell unless God through his grace saved us from our sins. This gloomy doctrine suggested damnation for the majority.

Another pivotal work was *The City of God*. This was written after the Visigoths sacked Rome in AD410 to rebut pagan charges that Rome's desertion of its old gods was to blame. Augustine essentially held that the kingdom of God was not of this world, although we ourselves have to live in it. Such beliefs were needed, for Augustine died as the Vandals – barbarians who deserved their infamy – besieged the city of Hippo.

NAMATIANUS (fl. AD404–16)

One of the last important non-Christian Roman poets, Namatianus (Claudius Rutilius Namatianus) came from Toulouse. Despite his paganism, Namatianus became Prefect of Rome under the (Christian) emperor Honorius.

Although he left Rome in AD416 soon after its sack by the Visigoths, Namatianus' parting poem expresses undimmed confidence in Rome's eternal glory. *Exaudi, regina tui pulcherrima mundi/Inter sidereos Roma recepta polos…* ("Listen, most beautiful queen of the world you have made your own. O Rome

received into the starry heavens,/Listen, O mother of gods and men.") There were to be no further such pagan panegyrics of the Eternal City.

BOETHIUS (*c.* AD480–526)

Although he was a Christian, Boethius (Amicus Manlius Severinus Boethius) never mentioned Christianity in his work. He came from an old aristocratic family, became consul in AD510 and then chief minister to Theodoric, king of the Ostrogoths, who was ruling Italy remarkably well. Boethius was implicated, probably unjustly, in a conspiracy against the king and sentenced to death. While in prison awaiting execution, he wrote *The Consolation of Philosophy* in a mixture of verse and prose. In this work, the most popular philosophical book in Western Europe for 1,000 years, Boethius drew on Platonist, Neoplatonist and Stoic ideas. He also provided much general intellectual knowledge that proved invaluable in the Middle Ages in a clear, classical Latin. He was the last such writer.

Below: This ancient Roman statue and the Pervigilium Veneris are both sensually beautiful invocations to Venus.

LITERATURE AND LITERACY

Above: A wall painting from Pompeii shows a young woman, once thought to be the Greek poet Sappho, pausing for thought.

Literacy was relatively widespread in the cities of the Roman empire, at least in the sense of being able to read and write the odd inscription, if not to read major pieces of literature. Despite the lack of a formal education system, especially beyond the primary level, for all but the children of a small elite – even they relied heavily on private tutors – it seems that many people in towns and cities were at least semi-literate, as the abundant graffiti and marks on potsherds (pottery fragments) or walls testify. These ordinary citizens were, however, only a minority of the empire's inhabitants. At least 80 per cent of the population were peasants.

A certain degree of literacy was essential for advancement in public life and very useful elsewhere, not just in the households of great nobles or in the imperial bureaucracy that very gradually grew out of the emperor's own household.

In the absence of printing technology, literate slaves and later monks painstakingly (and sometimes inaccurately) copied manuscripts. Cheap, convenient writing writing materials were also lacking. The two rival materials papyrus and parchment were both very expensive. (The Chinese are credited with inventing paper which was later adopted by Europe.) Instead, Romans had wax tablets, which were used and reused. While many citizens of the empire may have been literate, fewer probably had access to much literature. Few would have been able to read the Latin classics regularly or easily, for books or scrolls were very expensive in real terms. While papyrus fragments of Virgil's *Aeneid* found on Hadrian's Wall show that some knowledge of the classical canon was widespread, scrolls or books remained relatively few and much-cherished, lent only with caution even to close friends. Symmachus, the wealthy, cultured late 4th century AD Roman aristocrat, offered a would-be historian of Gaul his copy of Caesar's *Gallic Wars* only as a special favour.

ANCIENT LIBRARIES

Culture in the Graeco-Roman world remained overwhelmingly oral and declamation in public was the commonest means by which new books were published. (Traditionally, even the fully literate read everything aloud, though some historians now doubt this.) Both public and private libraries of any size were so few as to be noteworthy. In Pompeii, so far only one villa, the Villa of

Above: A 1st-century AD portrait from Pompeii shows the young Roman magistrate Terentius Nero and his wife. The image of the young couple pensively clutching writing materials reveals that women as well as men could read and write.

Below: Typical writing materials – a wooden tablet with three panels, a bronze inkwell and a stylus – from the 1st century AD. Papyrus, then the best writing material, was too expensive for most people for everyday use.

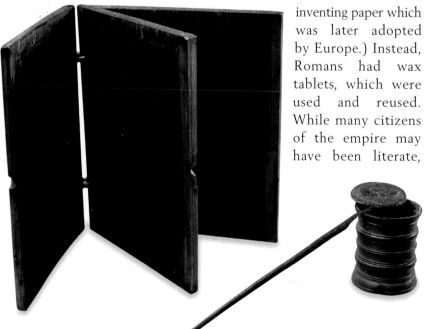

Right: The reconstructed interior of a typical Roman library such as those in Trajan's Forum, with shelves for the papyrus rolls.

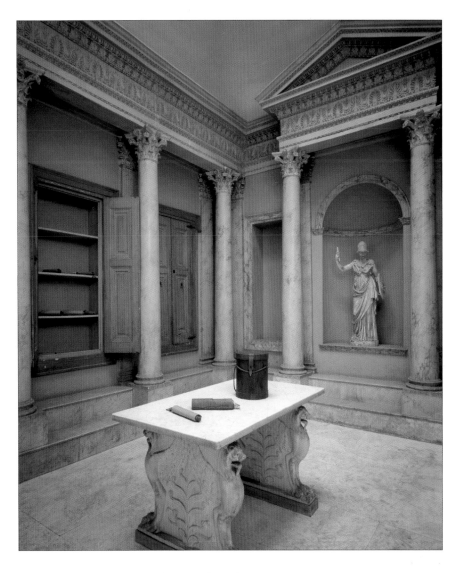

the Papyri, has been found to contain a significant number of scrolls. Although carbonized, they are slowly being deciphered. The emperor Gordianus III (AD238–44) reputedly had 60,000 tomes in his own library. This suggests a distinctly cultured emperor and was unusual enough to merit recording at the time.

The greatest library of the ancient world at Alexandria had around 500,000 volumes. Athens also had renowned public libraries. In the 2nd century AD, Rome reputedly had 39 libraries, although few if any of these were lending libraries. (The library behind Trajan's Basilica was divided into Greek and Latin sections.) Unlike public baths, aqueducts or amphitheatres, public libraries were not an automatic or even usual attribute of the typical Roman city. Ultimately, when urban life almost collapsed in the 5th and 6th centuries AD, monastic libraries became the chief repositories of Roman manuscripts. However, most Latin literature did not survive at all.

PAPYRUS v. PARCHMENT

The commonest way of writing in the Roman world before *c.* AD250 was on papyrus, made from the papyrus plant that grows abundantly only on the banks of the Nile. (Tiny amounts grow elsewhere, such as Syracuse, but this did not affect Egypt's monopoly, which also sustained its high price.) Papyrus was manufactured into scrolls up 25ft (8m) long. Unrolling such scrolls while reading was difficult – a slave's help was useful – and they were easily torn. More expensive than even the best paper today, papyrus was also more fragile and less durable.

The Romans did not use clay tablets for literary works, although bureaucratic records on clay tablets survive in some abundance from Egyptian and a few Mesopotamian sites. Parchment, made

from animal hides and far tougher than papyrus, was first made in the Hellenistic kingdom of Pergamum (Asia Minor). By the 1st century BC parchment sheets tied together with thongs were being used for commercial records. A century later, parchment was being used for literary texts as a *codex*, initially for cheaper editions. By AD200 this format was starting to replace papyrus scrolls.

The advent of Christianity in the 4th century AD accelerated this process. It was easier to find and read a passage from the Bible from a *codex* than a scroll and codices were also suited to legal documents. (Hence our term codex.) However, papyrus continued to be used until the Arab conquest of the Mediterranean in the 7th century AD finally cut Western Europe off from supplies in Egypt.

Below: A piece of papyrus signed by Cleopatra VII of Egypt, which dates to 33BC, gives tax benefits to the Roman Publius Candius.

THE ARTS

If Roman art was heavily indebted to the Greeks, it soon developed its own characteristics, especially in portraiture and in reliefs commemorating particular historic events. Among opposed artistic currents are those of native *veristic* (realistic) art versus idealised Greek art and metropolitan versus provincial. The art of classical Greece long epitomized perfection to Rome's ruling class (and to many artists) and was much copied. Augustus in particular employed classical art in the service of the state.

Sculpture has generally survived better than painting, in part because of its sheer quantity. In the 4th century AD it was claimed that the city of Rome contained as many statues as it did people. This was an exaggeration – there were perhaps 700,000 Romans – but contemporary surveys record 154 gold or ivory, 22 equestrian and 3,785 bronze statues. Few bronzes survive as valuable metal statues were melted down. Marble statues still intact have lost their paint, giving an unduly marmoreal impression today. Inevitably, these sculptures mostly depict the rich and powerful.

Fortunately for posterity, the eruption of Vesuvius in AD79 preserved the wall paintings of more ordinary houses in Pompeii and Herculaneum. Other murals unearthed from Nero's palace display imperial taste in the mid-1st century AD. Art became flamboyant under the Flavians, then came a Greek revival under Hadrian. By *c.* AD330, the long tradition of classical realism was giving way to the more stylized art that we call Byzantine.

Left: The arrival of Io in Egypt, a painting from the 1st century AD, shows Roman wall-painting in its prime, almost three-dimensionally realistic but also romantically poetic.

THE ETRUSCANS AND THE EARLY REPUBLIC

Little distinctively Roman art survives from the city's first centuries, when Rome was much influenced by its neighbours, the Etruscans. The latter, it is now accepted, were an indigenous Italian people like the Romans, not newcomers from Asia Minor as ancient legends suggest. In the 6th century BC they established a confederacy of 12 cities across central Italy. Their cultural influence extended south to the Bay of Naples and dominated Rome well after the traditional expulsion of King Tarquinius in 509BC that led to the founding of the Republic.

ETRUSCAN VIVACITY

While the Etruscans were wealthy, Rome itself probably became economically poorer in the 5th century BC. The Etruscans were induced by the Greek vases they imported to copy Greek legends as well as styles, but they did so with novel vigour and colour. Most of their statues were made of brightly painted terracotta (baked earth) rather than the marble and stone which were so abundant in Greece. The Etruscans were also formidable bronze smiths. Roman art was for a time little more than a variant of Etruscan and the artists themselves were probably often Etruscan.

Etruscan vivacity is manifest in the Apollo of Veii, taken from the temple of the Etruscan city that Rome captured in 396BC. Dating from c. 500BC, this life-size terracotta statue shows the god striding forward in a long flowing robe with an enigmatic "archaic" smile. The contrast with the still static *kouroi* (naked male figures) of contemporary Greek archaic art is marked but the Etruscans lacked the idealizing drive that was about to create Greek classical art. Although the Etruscan Apollo is walking, the upper part of his clothed body shows no real sign of movement, suggesting that the sculptor had not studied the nude body as the Greeks did. The statue, whose colours faintly survive, is the grandest of the terracotta statues that adorned the roofs of most

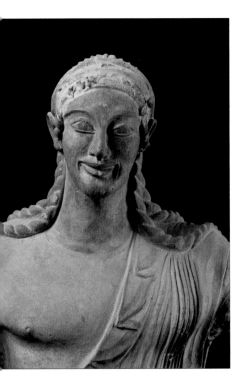

Above: The Apollo of Veii of c. 500BC, a terracotta masterpiece of Etruscan sculpture, shows Greek influence interpreted by Italian craftsmen. The enigmatic archaic smile is typical of statues of the time.

Right: The Wounded Chimaera of Arezzo, c. 380BC. This mythical creature, which bristles with almost electric menace, represents the peak of Etruscan bronze casting.

Etruscan and early Roman temples. A fine sarcophagus, from *c.* 500BC, which depicts the terracotta figures of a couple reclining connubially on top of their coffin, also comes from Veii. Later the Etruscans began to portray individuals more realistically, as in the limestone and stucco Urn of Arnth Velimnas from the Tomb of the Volumni in Perugia of *c.* 150BC. Arnth Velimnas is depicted with a paunch.

Probably the earliest statue in Rome itself is the Capitoline Wolf, a bronze dating from *c.* 500BC whose pointed teeth and jutting ribs still radiate feral savagery. The statue illustrates the myth of Rome's foundation, when a she-wolf suckled the abandoned divine twins Romulus and Remus. It could be the statue referred to by Cicero that was struck by lightning on the Capitoline, although the figures of the twins are Renaissance additions or replacements. Even more aggressive is the Wounded Chimaera from Arezzo of *c.* 380BC, a creature that in myth breathed fire and here bristles with electric menace. Both are superb examples of the early bronze working skills developed in Italy.

Roman artists also created fine busts or statues of prominent men, always a vital art in Rome. Unlike the Greeks, Roman artists normally concentrated on depicting the face, which from the start they portrayed more realistically. The finest surviving such statue from the earlier Republic is the so-called Brutus, once thought to portray the Roman noble who, according to legend, helped to expel the last Etruscan king. The bronze is now thought to date from *c.* 300BC, two centuries later, but it catches the determination, intelligence and dignity of a noble Roman. There is a thin-lipped grimness about the figure which is appropriate to the men who would lead Rome through the long trials of the Punic Wars.

Work such as this shows Greek influence creatively mediated by Italic veristic (realistic) traditions. This would become less possible after Rome's conquest of the rich Hellenistic world led highly skilled Greek artists to flood into the city.

ETRUSCAN TOMB PAINTING

The Etruscans' superb tomb paintings are interesting as little painting has survived from the ancient world outside Egypt. (According to Pliny the Elder, Fabius Pictor (Fabius the Painter) painted superb battle scenes inside the Temple of Salus in *c.* 300BC, but these are now lost.)

The Etruscan *Ambush of Troilus by Achilles* from the Tomb of the Bulls from Tarquinia in southern Tuscany illustrates a scene from Homer's *Iliad*. It reveals Etruscan knowledge of Greek culture and myth as early as 540BC. The technique used is dark silhouettes for most people and distinct outlines for Troilus' horse, the lions and the blocks of the fountain.

Another delightful tomb painting is that from the Tomb of Hunting and Fishing of the same period. It depicts birds and boys climbing rocks and diving.

From the Tomb of Orcus in the 4th century BC comes the profile of a beautiful woman called Velia, crowned with leaves and with her hair hanging loose. Greek classicism is evident here, but again mediated by Etruscan taste. All this is very far from the art trumpeting military or dynastic glories that was to become the Roman norm.

Above: The Ambush of Troilus by Achilles, from Tarquinia, is typical of c. 540BC. It shows the Etruscans' awareness of Greek myths and style but interprets both in their own distinctive manner.

Above: The so-called Brutus, a fine bronze statue from c. 300BC, shows Greek influences in its style but is very Roman in its subject matter: a dignified Roman nobleman of the sort who would soon have to face the threat of Hannibal.

ART IN THE LATER REPUBLIC: 211–31BC

Above: A fantasy city painted with almost perfect perspective in the bedroom of a villa at Boscoreale near Pompeii in the 1st century BC.

Below: The reliefs from the Temple of Neptune in Rome (formerly called the Altar of Domitius Ahenobarbus) mingle Greek style and Roman subject matter in a way very typical of the time, c. 100BC.

In 211BC the Roman general Marcellus captured and sacked Syracuse, the great Greek metropolis of the West, bringing home art treasures that bedazzled the Romans. "Before this Rome knew nothing of these exquisite refined things… rather it was full of barbaric weapons and bloody spoils of war", wrote Plutarch 300 years later. He was exaggerating but in the following decades Greek artworks indeed poured into Rome as its armies returned triumphant from the eastern Mediterranean. Corinth fell to Roman arms in 146BC and the sophisticated kingdom of Pergamum was bequeathed peacefully in 133BC.

ADAPTING GREEK STYLE

With the artworks came Hellenistic artists whose impact was for a time overwhelming (although the native veristic tradition of portraiture survived only marginally modified). Demand for Greek artworks among Roman nobles became so insatiable that artists began copying them in the often repetitive Neo-Attic style. Unlike their Greek originals, many such copies have survived.

Greek influence from southern Italy appears in the simple, elegant Ionic *volutes* (scrolls) of the Sarcophagus of Lucius Cornelius Scipio *c.* 200BC. The first relief depicting a Roman historical event is the marble frieze of the monument to Aemilius Paullus at Delphi in Greece, which was erected after his victory at Pydna in 168BC. It features a specific event from the battle – a bolting riderless horse – in a way that is typically Roman although Greek artists sculpted it. Paullus brought back to Rome the Athenian painter Metrodoros, one among many imported Greek artists.

The famous reliefs in marble from the Temple of Neptune in Rome (once called the Altar of Domitius Ahenobarbus) of *c.* 100BC mingle Greek and Roman motifs. Three sides depict the usual mythological scenes – the wedding of Amphitrite and Neptune for example – with typical Hellenistic flair, but the fourth shows a mundane scene of Roman census-taking. This is handled more awkwardly as the unknown artist(s) struggled to adapt Greek style to Roman demands for commemorative works. It is possible that this last side was added to an existing altar.

A less happy adaptation of Greek styles was the practice of putting Roman portrait heads on to idealized Greek statues. The so-called Pseudo-athlete, in which the head of an Italian businessman of *c.* 80BC tops the heroic torso of a Greek athlete, is typical. The middle-aged Roman has the head of a clearly older man and a well muscled torso with drapery around the hips. Equally ridiculous was the way some Roman magnates allowed themselves to be portrayed as Hellenistic god-kings in emulation of Alexander the Great. Pompey, hailed as a god on his victorious march through the Hellenistic East (66–62BC), was portrayed with an Alexander-style quiff that sits like a wig above his middle-aged Roman features.

Balancing this uncritical importation of things Greek was the veristic style favoured by more conservative Romans who had no taste for fancy foreign art and who preferred styles that reflected older Republican virtues. Instead, they favoured an almost excessively realistic portraiture style that emphasizes every wrinkle and furrow, such as the "Republican portraits" from the mid-1st century. These portraits may have been taken from the death masks many Romans kept in their homes for the worship of ancestors.

POMPEIIAN ART: THE FIRST STYLES

The small but wealthy cities of Pompeii and Herculaneum in Campania, near Naples, were very open to Greek influences. They have the best preserved Roman mosaics and wall-paintings, although similar paintings have been found in Rome itself. The consecutive decorative styles of wall painting have been labelled the First, Second, Third and Fourth Pompeian styles. The First Pompeian style emerged in the 2nd century BC. Generally simple, it used plaster moulded and painted to look like coloured marble or stone.

The Second Pompeian Style that developed after 80BC was more interesting. It used realistically painted architectural features to create almost three-dimensional effects. The Villa of Oplontis, which belonged to Poppaea, Nero's second wife, boasts a remarkable vista – a colonnade behind a peacock and theatrical mask – that approaches true trompe l'oeil. The bedroom of the villa at Boscoreale has murals that show gardens or fantastic

buildings that never existed except in the unknown artist's imagination. The aptly named Villa of the Mysteries, however, shows rituals from a real Dionysiac mystery cult, with life-size figures that seem to stand or move on painted ledges in real space. This copies Greek *megalography* (large-scale figure painting). In a house on the Esquiline Hill in Rome, wall paintings of *c.* 50BC illustrate scenes from the *Odyssey* that use atmospheric perspective to increase the illusion of distance in the dream-like landscapes.

Mosaics, made by pressing small stones and pieces of glass or marble into a soft mortar bedding, were used widely by the Romans but had been used in the Hellenistic world too. The renowned Alexander Mosaic from the House of the Faun in Pompeii probably copies a Greek painting done by Philoxenos of *c.* 300BC. It may have been imported from Greece in the 1st century BC, but it is more likely that it was the craftsman who was imported. About 17 by 9ft (5.2 by 2.7m), it creates illusory real space to depict the drama of the Battle of Issus (333BC), when Alexander almost captured the Persian king Darius II.

Above: In the Villa at Oplontis near Pompeii, which belonged to the empress Poppaea, the illusionism of the Second Pompeian Style, c. 50BC, is fully manifested, with the pillars receding dramatically into the distance.

Below: A fresco from the Hall of the Mysteries, in the Villa of the Mysteries at Pompeii, showing an initiate to the Dionysian cult weeping.

AUGUSTUS AND THE CLASSICAL REVIVAL: 31BC–AD64

Above: A cameo showing an ageless Augustus in dignified profile. Such images had strong propaganda purposes, as the medieval emperor Lothair realized when he incorporated it in his crown.

Below: A sacro-idyllic landscape of the type which first emerged in the Third Pompeian Style. Supposedly depicting country shrines, in fact they offered the artists opportunities to create imaginary landscapes of a type not seen again until the Renaissance.

After defeating his rival Mark Antony at Actium in 31BC, Augustus (as Octavian was known after 27BC) declared a policy of *restitutio rei publicae*. This meant a return to stable, constitutional, above all peaceful government. Art, architecture and literature were all enrolled in a highly successful propaganda campaign to proclaim the advent of a golden age after a century of civil strife.

EMBODYING ROMAN *VIRTUS*
Augustus looked back to the art of classical Athens at its 5th century BC peak for an authority, perfection and calm that appealed to him both personally and politically. (He did not of course emulate Athenian democracy, but Rome had never been truly democratic.) The result, which marked the first classical revival, was far more original than most Neo-Attic art had been, for Augustus used Athenian forms for most un-Athenian ends: his portrayal as the supreme embodiment of Roman *virtus*, the archetypal Roman virtue of courage, excellence, piety and strength.

Virtus is very obvious in the statue of the Prima Porta Augustus (so-called after the villa where it was found, which had once belonged to the empress Livia). Possibly a copy of a lost bronze, it dates from *c.* 20BC, and was originally painted with lifelike colours.

A still youthful-looking Augustus is shown, larger than life, as a triumphant *imperator* (emperor/general) in ceremonial armour. On his breastplate, personifications of the sky, Caelus, and of the sun, Sol, at the top are balanced by the figure of Tellus, the earth, reclining at the bottom. Around them are other deities, including Diana and Apollo. Between them Augustus is shown receiving the legionary standards lost at the battle of Carrhae in 53BC from a baggy-trousered Parthian. This refers to a recent diplomatic triumph (20–19BC) and links the mythical and the political. At Augustus' feet a cupid emphasizes the claimed descent of his family, the Julians, from Venus through her son Aeneas, while the dolphin the cupid rides recalls his naval victory at

Actium. The whole statue is therefore loaded with political significance. Augustus' stance is modelled on the nude *Doryphoros* (spear-carrier), a statue by the great Athenian sculptor Polyclitus of *c.* 450BC.

Another, less idealized statue shows Augustus with his toga over his head in the role of a priest (he became Pontifex Maximus, supreme priest, in 12BC). Augustus is, as always depicted as boyishly youthful but here he is also solemnly pious. His features are typically classical – smooth skin, regular features, sharp-edged nose and brow – suggesting calm, benign authority. The same classical dignity pervades the bust of his grand-daughter Agrippina, wife and then widow of Germanicus, the popular general whom Tiberius allegedly harassed. There is a strong facial resemblance to her grand-father in a bust of *c.* AD30.

The Gemma Augusta, a cameo showing the dead and deified Augustus passing power to his successor Tiberius from *c.* AD20, perpetuates this fine classicism. However, later statues of the Julio-Claudians, such as that depicting the ungainly emperor Claudius as Jupiter, are less successful.

Perhaps the greatest achievement of Augustan sculptors was the Ara Pacis Augusti (Altar of Augustan Peace). Constructed between 13 and 9BC and dedicated on the empress Livia's birthday, it is set in a walled enclosure with its main decorations on the outer walls. These are about 34ft long by 38ft wide (10.5 by 11.6m). Their message is that Augustus has restored peace, piety and prosperity and their form is sublimely classical. A sculptural panel on the east side portrays a personification the earth Tellus (or of Italia or Peace), with fruits and babies on her lap to symbolize fertility, flanked by two female figures symbolizing the oceans and rivers. The inspiration came from a Greek 5th-century relief, the Stele of Hegesos. Similarly, the famous frieze of the Panathenaic Procession from the Parthenon in Athens probably inspired the imperial procession on the side walls of the altar. Here Augustus is portrayed as *pater patriae* (father of his country). He takes centre stage without overwhelming his friends and family, including the empress Livia. Small boys, his grandsons, clutch at the grown-ups' hands, adding a homely touch. This reveals the Principate at its height, dignified yet family-minded. Another relief shows Aeneas, renowned for his piety, sacrificing to the *penates*, the household gods that he had brought from Troy.

WALL PAINTINGS

The Second Pompeian Style continued after 31BC. Livia's house on the Palatine is decorated with marvellous murals of gardens, while another house, now beneath the Villa Farnesina, had walls painted with remarkable trompe l'oeil to resemble a picture gallery. Outline paintings, such as one from this villa showing a woman pouring perfume, recall classical Greek art's sublime simplicity.

The succeeding Third Pompeian Style, which emerged at the end of the 1st century BC, was less solidly illusionistic. It treated walls as flat surfaces rather than as windows. Painted columns became slimmer, holding up delicate ornamental pediments. This style also saw the first emergence of "sacro-idyllic landscapes", romanticized misty landscapes centred supposedly on a shrine or temple but in reality rejoicing in vistas dotted with bridges, rocks and shepherds' huts, with mountains in the vague distance. While perhaps influenced by Hellenistic precursors, these are among the finest and earliest of European landscapes.

Right: The Prima Porta statue of Augustus c. 20BC, a copy of a lost bronze. The ever-youthful emperor is in symbolic armour proclaiming the Parthian victory, while the Cupid at his feet hints at descent from Venus. All is nobly classical.

Above: Official Augustan art looked back to classical Athenian precedents in works such as the Ara Pacis Augusti (the Altar of Peace of Augustus) finished 9BC. Tellus, the personified earth, has fruit and babies on her lap and is flanked by rivers.

THE ROMAN ZENITH:
FROM NERO TO TRAJAN AD64–117

Right: A gouache copy of one of the now-faded wall paintings discovered in Nero's Domus Aurea, illustrating the elegant Fourth Pompeian Style which once decorated it. Architectural elements are colourfully mixed with the illusionistic Second Style.

Below: The playboy-emperor and would-be artist Nero, unflatteringly portrayed with curled hair and a double chin although still in his twenties.

In AD64 the great fire that destroyed most of Rome also allowed Nero, now unrestrained by his old tutor Seneca and his first Praetorian Prefect Burrus, to give free rein to his far from classical tastes. Although Nero was deposed four years later and his final successor Vespasian favoured a more popular art, the fifty years following the fire saw Roman art flourish as never before. Hellenistic influences were finally absorbed and the empire's wealth allowed a dynamic, almost baroque yet Roman style to emerge. The eruption of Vesuvius, from the archaeologist's viewpoint, provided a blessed preservative.

The murals of Nero's Domus Aurea (Golden Palace), which were fresh when rediscovered by Renaissance artists – Raphael crawled down into the "grottoes"

to admire them – have sadly faded but still give a good example of the Fourth Pompeian Style. This continues the Third Style but reverts also to more solid, illusionistic architectural elements of the Second Style in a fanciful manner.

THE FOURTH POMPEIAN STYLE

In Pompeii, superb examples of the Fourth style come from the House of the Vettii brothers – probably merchants – which was rebuilt after a major earthquake in AD62. Copies of famous Greek paintings of legends – the death of King Pentheus, the baby Hercules strangling snakes – were incorporated as painted panels within wall decorations. The painting of Achilles and Briseis, a scene from the *Iliad*, in the House of the Tragic Poet is also impressive. Achilles smoulders with half-suppressed wrath as his favourite slave-girl Briseis is led away for King Agamemnon's pleasure. Other Pompeian paintings treat everyday subjects and reveal that local artists could paint diverse subjects with equal skill. This window on to life in antiquity closed in August AD79.

NERO'S SUCCESSORS

Sculpture and relief carvings remained the favoured forms of official art, prominently displayed in cities across the empire. Along with each emperor's coins, they carried the imperial image and official messages, although the effects may not have always been exactly what their imperial propagators envisaged. The statues and coins of Nero (ruled AD54–68) reveal more of his character – part debauched buffoon, part genuine aspiring artist, very seldom competent emperor – than he probably realized, with fleshy double chin and grandiose laurel crowns to proclaim his "victories" in the Olympic Games where he carried off every prize.

The busts and coins of his successor Vespasian, already 60 and a fine general when he gained the throne, are very different. Bald, unbeautiful but earthily humorous – on his deathbed he joked, "I think I must be becoming a god", referring to an emperor's customary posthumous deification – his features are shown in a revived veristic style.

Titus, Vespasian's handsome, young and prodigal son and heir, trumpeted his triumph over the Jews whose revolt he had crushed with flamboyant reliefs on his arch. The nearest figures in the imperial entourage, which include Titus himself in his four-horsed chariot with a winged Victory behind him, stand out in such high relief they are nearly in the round. These contrast with the lesser figures modelled in low relief but all, as usual in imperial art of this period, create the illusion of being in real space.

Under Trajan (ruled AD98–117), perhaps the most popular of emperors, Rome approached its zenith. His great column in Rome, erected in AD113 behind his Basilica, carries a brilliant spiral with some 2,500 figures showing his victory over the Dacians. Its scenes provide vivid (if not always wholly accurate) snapshots of the Roman army in action as it crossed rivers, stormed forts and tended its wounded. Panels from the Arch of Trajan erected at Benevento AD114–17 in southern Italy show the humanitarian ruler distributing food to poor children and presiding over the construction of a new port near Ostia, all facets of a great ruler.

THE PLEBEIAN TRADITION

Not all surviving Roman art is imperial or aristocratic. The Tomb of the Haterii of *c.* AD100 was commissioned by a non-aristocratic Roman family, who were probably successful builders. Here attention is lavished on details of the building, a family mausoleum under construction. A disregard for perspective and a delight in rich, almost fussy ornamentation shows that this sort of popular art remained blithely unconcerned with the nobility's favoured classical naturalism and idealism.

Above: The native Italian veristic tradition was revived for this bust of Vespasian, the emperor who came from small-town Italy. It shows him as realistically bald and elderly, but wryly humorous.

Below: A scene from the Tomb of the Haterii, probably erected for a family of rich builders c. AD90, shows a taste for rich ornamentation far removed from upper-class ideals of naturalism.

HADRIAN AND THE GREEK REVIVAL: AD117–285

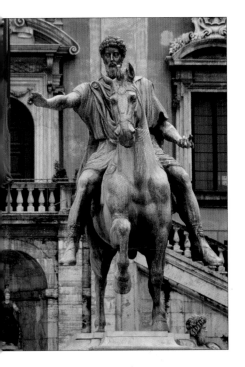

Above: The statue of Marcus Aurelius, the only surviving bronze equestrian statue from antiquity, AD164–6.

Below: Along with the multicoloured mosaics, the 2nd century AD saw very fine black-and-white mosaics, such as this floor at Ostia.

Although the emperor Hadrian displayed architectural radicalism in the Pantheon in Rome and in his villa at Tivoli, he was conservative in his choice of artworks, favouring a return to classical or even earlier Greek styles. This second Classical Revival derived not just from his personal tastes, for the century saw the emergence of what is termed the Second Sophistic. This attempted to revive some aspects of classical Greek life – cities even began debating political issues of the 5th century BC – as Greek provinces finally regained some of their prosperity and self-confidence after the devastation wrought by Rome's conquest and civil strife.

ART AT HADRIAN'S VILLA

At Tivoli, 20 miles (32km) from Rome, Hadrian filled his villa complex with numerous statues, mostly reproductions of famous Greek or Egyptian works, to remind him of his travels. His decorators also created superb mosaics such as that showing a battle between centaurs and wild beasts based on a Greek work by Zeuxis of *c.* 400BC. On his travels Hadrian fell in love with Antinous, a beautiful youth of royal birth from Bithynia, who accompanied him until he was drowned in the Nile in AD130. To commemorate him, the grief-stricken emperor founded a city on the Nile (besides more enduring foundations such as Hadrianopolis, now Edirne in Turkey) and "set up statues of him, or rather cult images, throughout the entire inhabited world", according to the historian Dio Cassius. Greek artists made statues showing Antinous as Apollo, Bacchus, Hermes and Osiris. If his body is truly Hellenic, he often has a most unclassical pout.

The Baths of Neptune in Ostia at the Tiber's mouth had a fine mosaic floor in black and white. Completed in AD139, it showed mythical sea-creatures – tritons, hippocamps, nereids – circling around the sea-god. The lack of colour brings out the fine draughtsmanship and this style remained popular into the 4th century.

Far to the north a remarkable fresco has been found in Southwark, across the Thames from Roman London, dating from *c.* AD150. It used very expensive pigments – gold leaf and cinnabar – to revive or perpetuate the Third Pompeian Style. Slender pillars supporting delicate pediments provide evidence that Roman wealth and sophistication had reached even this remote province.

One of the greatest of all Roman artworks is the sole surviving Roman equestrian bronze statue of Marcus Aurelius – preserved because it was thought to depict Constantine, the first Christian emperor – which was erected AD164–6. The philosopher-emperor is shown in heavy tunic and cloak as a general, his arm raised as if addressing a crowd, but his features retain a thoughtful, nobly compassionate air.

Above: The debauched megalomania of Commodus, shown dressed as Hercules, is wonderfully conveyed in this decadent bust.

A different, world-weary tone dominates the column of Marcus Aurelius of AD180–92, where the horrors of war are vividly portrayed. In comical contrast, the full-size naked portrait of Lucius Verus reveals the vanity of Marcus' idle co-emperor. The bust of Commodus, Marcus' worthless heir, dressed as Hercules with lionskin and club, is another masterly portrait, revealing the debauched megalomania of the last of the Antonines.

SEVERAN ART
A new art began to emerge with the succeeding dynasty, the Severans (AD193–233). This partly rejected Graeco-Roman classicism for a more stylized art. However, the two approaches long co-existed (as the classical and veristic traditions had for centuries) and often mixed. There is a florid exuberance about the busts of Septimius Severus (first of the dynasty), whose elaborately curled beard and hairstyle sit oddly with the ruthless face of a general who destroyed two rivals to gain the throne. The busts

of the following period are increasingly in the veristic tradition and that of the brutal emperor Caracalla (ruled AD211–17) is almost alarmingly realistic. Most of his successors, such as Maximinus Thrax or Trebonianus Gallus, cultivated this thuggish look as the empire disintegrated into chaos. Only the emperor Gallienus (ruled AD253–68) reverted to a noble, spiritual air. This was well-suited to a ruler who patronized the unworldly philosopher Plotinus and lost much of the empire.

SARCOPHAGI
One art form that developed steadily even in troubled times was the sarcophagus. This reflected the growing trend towards inhumation (burial) rather than cremation from Hadrian's reign on, and provided great opportunities for Attic (Greek) sculptors. In the 2nd century AD, these sarcophagi have fine classical carvings, often of Greek legends unconnected with the deceased's life. Typical is the sarcophagus of AD190 showing the scene from the *Iliad* of the corpse of prince Hector being dragged around the walls of Troy. Others combine myth with personal touches, such as the sarcophagus from AD250 showing a couple reclining together in death on the lid and legendary scenes from Achilles at the court of Lycomedes round the sides.

A rival to the Attic school of sarcophagi sculptors was the Asiatic school. Here too mythological scenes in a classical style decorated the sides of sarcophagi, but columns divide the scenes. A particularly elaborate example is dated *c*. AD180. Now in Melfi Cathedral in southern Italy, although its original occupant was pagan, it has *aediculae* (pavilions) on all four sides with mythological figures in each and a door at one end. The deceased's carved image reclines on top. Such pagan funeral imagery continued well into the Christian empire.

Right: Hadrian's beautiful lover Antinous, who died mysteriously in the Nile, was portrayed in many different poses.

Above: Under the new African dynasty started by Septimius Severus in AD193, new forms of less classical art emerged, often more stylized but not wholly displacing classicism.

ART OF THE LATER EMPIRE:
AD285–535

With the advent of Diocletian in AD284, the troubled empire entered a new, more stable but more politically restricted era. Roman art reflected this as earlier trends away from classical idealism and its accompanying naturalism intensified. Instead, there emerged an art that aimed at creating overwhelmingly imposing images of imperial power, turned inward away from a collapsing natural world. This makes later Roman art effectively a bridge to that of the Byzantine and medieval world.

Above: The grim determination of the four tetrarchs (co-rulers) is graphically revealed in this unusual statue of c. AD305, now built into St Mark's, Venice, but originally from Constantinople.

Below: Constantine I favoured an art that overwhelmed the onlooker in its size and majesty. This head, once part of a huge statue, is 8ft 6in (2.6m) high.

THE STYLE OF POWER

Diocletian and his successors tried to exalt the imperial throne so far above its subjects that none would dare to challenge it. While this aim had limited success politically, it had huge repercussions aesthetically. The statues of the tetrarchs (four co-rulers) embracing in St Mark's, Venice, of c. AD305 reveal the new order's grim determination and also the tetrarchs' astonishing lack of individuality – their features are almost interchangeable. However, the real power of the new style is seen best in the giant head and hands of Constantine, all that remain of a colossal seated statue of the emperor that once stared down on observers in the Basilica Nova in Rome. The head alone is 8ft 6in (2.6m) high and the whole statue intact would have risen 30ft (9m). The huge eyes gaze out blankly yet all-seeingly on the subjects dwarfed below. The aquiline nose and clean-shaven jaw – Constantine was the first beardless emperor since Trajan – reinforce the feeling of sheer power which emanates from this superb piece of propaganda.

Less startlingly original was the Arch of Constantine. This partly reused Trajanic, Hadrianic and Antonine material but also has some new friezes. On two of these, panels showing Constantine delivering an oration or distributing gifts to the Roman people, the emperor stares out in grandiose isolation while his courtiers, lined up stiffly, gaze adoringly up towards him. The contrast with the classical realism of the two purloined Hadrianic roundels is striking. The change cannot be attributed simply to a decline in craftsmanship but must reflect a preference, emerging even before Constantine became Christian, for an art that was more hieratic and oppressive and less realistic and humanist than earlier official art. Man had ceased to be "the measure of all things", as he had been in classical Greece and Augustan Rome and now humbly genuflected before awesomely distant imperial – or divine – majesty. All the earlier panels are re-worked so that the emperor looks like Constantine. As a result he sometimes has a very small head.

Later imperial monuments such as the base of the Obelisk of Theodosius I in Constantinople (Istanbul) of AD390–3 take yet further this process of magnifying imperial glory while reducing subjects to mere ciphers. The emperor is shown standing behind the imperial pavilion's railing with a wreath in his hand, while beside and below him his courtiers, reduced to rows of anonymous heads, gaze out full-frontally. (Severe weathering has probably accentuated this impression of impersonality.)

Better preserved is the superb silver dish some 2ft 5in (73.6cm) in diameter made in AD388 which shows Theodosius with his co-emperors Valentinian II and Arcadius, his son, all holding orbs to symbolize power. The co-emperors are portrayed smaller to indicate their lesser power. Theodosius is presenting something to an official, who is shown far smaller, befitting a man of lower status. Such symbolism marks a clean break with naturalistic classicism.

The most beautiful examples of Late Roman/Byzantine imperial art come from Ravenna, reconquered by the Latin-speaking but Eastern emperor Justinian (AD527–65). The mosaics at San Vitale which show him staring out, flanked by clergy and soldiers, are Byzantine in their full-frontal two-dimensionality against a flat gold background, although traces of classicism remain in their individually identifiable features.

Ravenna's mosaics mark the final transition to post-Roman medieval art, for the wars to regain Italy from the Goths wrecked the last of Roman civilization more thoroughly than the Goths could.

CLASSICAL SURVIVALS

Although the now Christian imperial court preferred the new unnaturalistic art for propaganda purposes, many educated pagan Romans long continued to favour some form of classical art. The Symmachus family, one of Rome's grandest noble families, commissioned ivory diptychs (two-leaved panels) in c. AD390. These depict pagan priestesses before a shrine to Bacchus and Jupiter in a style that consciously aimed to revive something of Augustan classicism.

In Britain, where villa life flourished in the first half of the 4th century AD, the superb mosaic, the Woodchester Great Pavement of c. AD350, shows Orpheus charming the beasts amid geometric patterns that recall a carpet. A similar subject is treated more naturalistically in the Littlecote villa near Hungerford of c. AD360. Even more dramatic is the Mildenhall Treasure, a superb silver dish about 2ft (61cm) in diameter that was buried around AD360 for safekeeping. It shows scenes of bacchic revelry with maenads and satyrs that in both spirit and form recall a far earlier art.

In Sicily, the remarkable mosaics depicting hunting and bathing from the Piazza Armerina villa of c. AD310–30 glow with truly pagan vitality, although their style has moved away from classicism to a less naturalistic if still vivid art.

Above: This 6th-century AD mosaic from Sant'Apollinare Nuovo in Ravenna of the Three Magi (Wise Men) is a marvellous example of Byzantine art.

Below: The joyful, exuberant colours of the mosaics of the Piazza Armerina Villa in Sicily show that, even in the early 4th century AD, not all art was concerned with depicting grim power.

FURNITURE

Above: A fresco of the 1st century BC showing a Roman banquet with the typical small, portable tripod table that was then common. These were usually richly decorated.

Below: A bronze Roman couch or bed probably from the 1st century AD. It would have had cushions and covers and a mattress of wooden slats and might have been used both for dining and for sleeping.

Roman furniture was rather sparse but often also surprisingly elegant and comfortable. It certainly surpassed anything Western Europe was to know again for the next thousand years.

As with so much else, there was a marked Greek or Hellenistic influence on much Roman furniture design. Furniture for all but the poorest was always decorated in some way, for minimalism was never a virtue in Roman eyes. Excavations at Pompeii and Herculaneum have been invaluable for revealing well-preserved examples of furniture from the late Republican and early Imperial periods (100BC–AD79). The styles greatly influenced Neoclassical European furniture of the late 18th and early 19th centuries. However, it is unlikely that Roman furniture design changed radically in the three centuries that followed the eruption of Vesuvius.

TABLES AND SEATING

The Romans seem to have used five different types of table. These were all of Greek origin and made of bronze or marble as much as wood. The tables could be rectangular with three or four legs, or round with three legs. These were often zoomorphic in form, with lions' paws or griffins' legs or even with legs formed with ithyphallic satyrs. Small bronze tripod tables with rims to prevent things falling off – very useful on uneven floors – were particularly popular. So, too, were square stone or marble tables with a single central leg. The latter design was particularly common in courtyards or gardens, where they might be fixed, but most other furniture could be moved around. Portable charcoal braziers, the chief source of heating in private houses around the Mediterranean, were an exception. (Hypocaust central heating remained a very rare, expensive luxury in private houses and was only used in certain parts of the house.) A particularly fine example of a bronze tripod brazier dates from the late 1st century BC. A masterpiece of Roman metalwork, its elaborate sphinxes reveal the brief fashion for things Egyptian following the victory at Actium in 31BC and the annexation of Egypt.

Couches were made mainly of wood. A rectangular frame held the mattress, which was supported by leather straps, webbing or wooden slats to make a firm bed. There seems to have been little difference between the couches used for dining and beds proper – in many houses the two were probably interchangeable. Traces of couches with leather sides and backs that may have had cushions have also been discovered. Headboards sometimes had ornaments in the form of bronze or brass animal heads and could be inlaid with ivory, silver or tortoiseshell. A couch with a relief of bones has been partially restored and is displayed in the Fitzwilliam Museum, Cambridge.

The Romans had many different types of seating. Benches were generally considered poor people's seating and were made of wood or stone. Elaborate chairs, sometimes with arms and back supports, are shown in Roman sculptures and paintings. Heavy, ceremonial chairs with solid sides were used for official occasions. There is a carving from Trier of what looks like an armchair made of wicker in which a teacher sits instructing his students and a bronze-sheathed wooden chair leg has been found at Pompeii. Stools were widely used. A *sella curulis* (folding stool) with curving crossed legs was used by magistrates on official occasions. They were also used domestically; a relief from Ostia shows a woman seated under a tree on such a stool and Pompeii has produced a fine bronze-legged example. Thrones are usually shown with footstools.

CUPBOARDS AND LAMPS

Roman cupboards, cabinets and chests were generally similar to modern ones. A remarkably fine wooden cupboard cum shrine has been found in Herculaneum. The shrine at the top takes the form of a little temple, with finely carved Corinthian colonnettes (mini-columns) at its corners, and housed the statues of the household gods, the Lares and Penates. The cupboard below contained glassware and ornaments.

Discoveries at Herculaneum have shown that many rooms had wooden shutters or partitions that have normally left no archaeological record. These could be elaborate, folding, multi-panelled affairs with doors in them. External shutters were made of solid wood. It is clear from literature, painting and sculpture that large curtains would also have been used to divide rooms, but none have survived.

LAMPS

Roman houses were lit by lamps which burned olive oil. These ranged from very simple earthenware dishes to elaborate bronze stands. The simplest of these bronze lamp stands was a slender fluted column that rested on three animal paws and was topped by some form of calyx (flower top). Far more complicated were those with four or more arms, shaped either like branches or in the form of *volutes* (scroll-like ornaments). A particularly resplendent example comes

from the House of Diomedes at Pompeii. Dating from just before AD79, the lampstand rests on a platform decorated with a figure of a satyr riding a panther. The feet of the base are shaped like animal's paws.

Above: A woman seated at her toilette in a wicker armchair from near Trier in Gaul, 4th century AD. A servant holds a mirror in front of her.

Above: An elaborate Roman strong box for money and other valuables. Decorated with classical motifs and very fine lion legs, it probably dates from the 4th century AD.

RELIGION AND MYTHOLOGY

The Romans had many gods and, like most other polytheists, normally accepted those of other peoples. Most Greek gods were identified with Roman ones early on but, as Rome's power spread east, stranger gods found followers in the multiracial city: Cybele from Asia Minor, Isis and Sarapis from Egypt, Mithras from the Persian world. Their cults, which offered initiates mystical experiences and usually promised salvation after death, appealed especially to poorer people in the empire. In contrast, the official religion of the Roman establishment was essentially pragmatic and utilitarian. Worship involved precise rituals to ensure that the gods brought victory in battle or that they saved Rome from plague.

From Augustus' time on, the worship of the emperor, whose *genius* or divinity was linked with Roma Dea, the goddess of Rome, was encouraged. This imperial cult helped to unite the disparate empire and was vigorously enforced in the troubled 3rd century AD. The Jews were exempt because of the antiquity of their religion, but Christians suffered for their refusal to worship the emperor. Christianity's final triumph was due chiefly to its promotion by Constantine after AD312. But, as the Roman empire became Christian, Christianity in turn became imperially Roman.

Left: A scene thought to show the mystery rites of Bacchus (Dionysus) in a mural from the Villa of the Mysteries, Pompeii, c. 60–50BC. Note the goatlike ears of the left-hand figures.

THE CAPITOLINE GODS

The gods of early Rome were not initially anthropomorphic but, after 250BC, under increasing Greek influence, they soon acquired human characteristics. They were given mythical fixed forms like the 12 Greek Olympian gods by the poet Ennius. However, although myth and religion intertwined, religious fervour was not appropriate to the worship of Rome's state gods. Instead, punctilious performance of the rites was all-important.

Rome did not have a separate priestly caste or profession, although there were four priestly colleges by the late Republic. The *pontifices* were pre-eminent, while the *augures* divined the gods' will by observing the flight of birds or animals' entrails. Important Romans performed priestly duties as required, pulling their togas over their heads to indicate sacerdotal functions. The emperors from Augustus on became *pontifex maximus*, supreme priest, a title the Pope inherited.

The sacrifice of animals was central to the gods' worship. The animal entrails were examined for omens, an Etruscan habit which the Romans perpetuated. The best portions of the sacrifice were burnt as offerings to the gods and the priests and worshippers would eat the rest. Offerings of flowers or cakes were acceptable from poorer people and for lesser endeavours.

The temple of a pagan god was its house, not a place where worshippers gathered for collective rites. These rites were normally performed outside the temple. On special occasions the statue of the deity might be paraded through the streets, a custom still performed with Catholic statues on feast days. Jupiter, his wife Juno and his daughter Minerva, who sprang from his head fully grown and fully armed, formed the central Capitoline triad. However, Mars, the war god, was equally important.

JUPITER

The king of the gods, equated with Zeus (though lacking the Greek god's colourful sex life or touchy temper), Jupiter was a sky god associated with thunder, lightning, rainfall and storms. He used to warn men and punished them with his three thunder bolts when required. The first he could discharge as a warning whenever he wanted; the second, also a premonitory bolt, could be hurled with the agreement of the 12 other gods, his *complices*. The last, destroying bolt could only be unleashed by the god with the consent of the *superiores*, the hidden superior gods.

At first the god of a rustic Rome, Jupiter Elicius (Who Brings Forth) was concerned with farming, but as Rome's power grew, so did his. Called Jupiter Imperator (Supreme General), Invictus (Unconquered) and Triumphator, his highest title was Jupiter Optimus Maximus (Best and Greatest).

In his temple on the Capitoline, Jupiter was portrayed majestically, bearded, with an eagle on a sceptre and thunderbolts. Long the supreme god of the Roman

Above: The goddess Minerva, third of the Capitoline triad, from Souedia in Syria. Less obviously Roman than the other two, this patron of doctors and craftsmen was revered for her wisdom and widely worshipped.

Right: Thetis appealing to Jupiter in a painting by Ingres, 1811. The assimilation of such Greek deities into the Roman pantheon happened very early in Rome's history.

Left: The Capitoline triad; Jupiter, king of the gods, is flanked by his wife Juno, seated on his left with her peacock and Minerva, seated on his right with her owl, a symbol of wisdom. Temples to the Capitoline triad were built in cities such as Carthage around the empire.

state, senators declared war under his aegis and triumphant generals would donate a gold crown and part of their booty to him. The *Ludi Romani*, the chief games, were celebrated in his honour.

The Temple of Jupiter on the Capitoline Hill, which was built under the kings and rebuilt many times, was the grandest in the city of Rome. The rise of the cult of Sol Invictus (Unconquered Sun) eclipsed Jupiter's primacy in the 3rd century, but Diocletian (ruled AD284–305) revived Jupiter's glory, calling himself and his soldiers *Joviani*. Finally, the Christians adopted Jupiter's title of Optimus Maximus for their own god.

JUNO
The consort and sister of Jupiter, equated with the Greek goddess Hera, Juno was the supreme goddess of the Roman state and of very ancient origins. A statue of Juno was taken from the captured Etruscan city of Veii in 394BC and installed in Rome in a form of religious annexation, but she had been worshipped in Rome long before. A temple to her was built on the Esquiline Hill in 735BC.

As Juno Lucetia she was a goddess of light, a moon goddess. Traditionally shown with a peacock and sceptre as *regina coeli*, queen of heaven, her sacred geese on the Capitol warned the Romans of a night attack by the Gauls during their sack of Rome in 390BC. She was also the mother of Mars, although not by Jupiter but by union with a magic flower. Above all, Juno embodied the virtues of Roman matronhood, which were much respected in the Republic. As Juno Lucina she was goddess of childbirth and fertility – the Sabine women prayed to her after their rape by Romulus and his gang. As Juno Pronuba she presided over marriage and as Populonia she encouraged the Romans to multiply. The month of June is named after her.

MINERVA
Although identified with Athene, patron goddess of Athens and daughter of Zeus, Minerva was originally the Etruscan goddess Menrfa or Menarva (associated with an owl) and the least Roman of the Capitoline triad. At first the goddess of commerce, industry and education, she later became a warrior-goddess, depicted with helmet, shield and armour. Later still she also became the patron goddess of doctors, musicians and craftsmen and, in a typical example of Roman assimilation, was equated with the local goddess of Bath's hot springs, Sulis, in Britain. Her festival was celebrated in the Quinquatrus with Mars at the spring equinox.

Below: The Roman goddess Juno, who was generally portrayed as majestically imperious while embodying the sound virtues of Roman matronhood. She was identified with the Greek goddess Hera but she was far less temperamental.

Above: Mars, the helmeted god of war, was a deity of central importance to the all-conquering Romans.

Below: Apollo, god of music, poetry, medicine and science, shown with his lyre, was a Roman import from Greece who was fully assimilated into the state religion by Augustus.

MARS

The war god Mars was perhaps the most truly Roman of the city's gods and his cult was more important to Rome even than Jupiter's. At first he was a rustic deity living in fields and forests, called Silvanus. Later, Ceres and Liber, deities of wheat and wine, took over these agricultural roles but Mars' chief festival was always celebrated at the Quinquatrus at the spring equinox in the month that bears his name.

Born almost parthenogenetically from Juno's mystical union with a fantastic flower, he was identified with Ares but was a nobler and more dignified figure than the often irascible Greek god. At Rome he had a *sacrarium* (shrine) on the Palatine, where his 12 sacred spears were kept. His grandest temple in Rome was that built by Augustus to him as Mars Ultor, Mars the Avenger, to celebrate victory over Julius Caesar's assassins. The Romans built temples to him across the empire, in which he was generally portrayed bearded with helmet and armour. Sacrifices were made to him by generals before they set out for battle and after their victory he received his share of booty. On the battlefield he might appear accompanied by Pavor and Pallor (terror and paleness) which he inflicted on Rome's enemies, while his other two companions, Honos and Virtus, filled Roman soldiers with honour and courage. In the Romance languages Tuesday (Martes, Martedi, Mardi) is named after Mars.

APOLLO

The archetypal Greek god of poetry, medicine, music and science, Apollo had no Roman equivalent but was imported into the city in the 5th century BC to ward off plague. The dictator Camillus promised Apollo a tenth of the spoils from the Etruscan city of Veii, which Rome captured in 396BC, for Apollo was honoured also by the Etruscans.

Apollo was the son of Zeus (but not of Jupiter) and the titaness Leto. His twin sister was Artemis/Diana. Born on the island of Delos, Apollo slew the dragon Python at only four days old. Renamed as Delphi, the spot where the slaying took place later became the site of his oracle, the most sacred in the Greek world. Called Phoebus (brilliant), Apollo was a god of light and was later sometimes identified with the sun. Augustus built a fine temple near his house on the Palatine to the god whose lucid virtues he tried to propagate and many more were built across the empire.

DIANA

The goddess of the hunt and of the moon, later equated with Artemis and so Apollo's twin, Diana was the patron goddess of wild beasts. She was also associated with the moon, especially the harvest moon, for she was a fertility goddess. In her great temple at Ephesus in Asia Minor she was shown as many-breasted.

Diana undoubtedly had a savage temper. When Actaeon the hunter chanced upon her bathing with her nymphs, she angrily changed him into a stag and he was then killed by his own dogs. At Rome Diana

Left: Diana the chaste goddess, portrayed as a huntress on a 2nd-century AD mosaic from North Africa. In this guise Diana was virginal and almost amazonian, in contrast to more typically feminine goddesses.

was worshipped as a goddess of childbirth in a temple on the Aventine founded in the 6th century BC. Her greatest shrine was on the shores of Lake Nemi north of Rome, where her priest was traditionally an escaped slave. To win this priesthood he had to kill his predecessor in single combat, after which he had to patrol the lake's forested shores looking out for potential successors.

SATURN

An ancient agricultural god whose name was connected with *satur* (literally: stuffed), Saturn was identified with the Greek god Cronus. Expelled from heaven by Jupiter, Saturn was held to have ruled Italy during its golden age before the invention of iron and war. Saturday is named after Saturn.

Saturn's annual festival, the Saturnalia, which took place between the 17th and 23rd of December, saw an orgy of merriment when all rules were relaxed, the Lord of Misrule governed, masters waited upon their slaves and huge public banquets were eaten in the open. Saturn's temple in the Forum Romanum housed the public treasury and the standards of legions not actually campaigning. It was also a very early shrine of the Republic dating from *c.* 494BC.

VESTA AND THE VESTAL VIRGINS

Vesta was goddess of the domestic hearth and sown fields. She was linked with the Greek goddess Hestia, a notably chaste goddess. In Rome she was served by six patrician girls who were chosen by lot at the age of six. They were required to serve for 30 years from the age of ten in the special Atrium Vestae, the House of the Vestals next to the circular Temple of Vesta in the Forum Romanum. After that time they were free to marry, although few did, as they were considered too old. The Vestal Virgins were, however, much respected. Their main duty was to keep the goddess's sacred flame burning, and their chief restriction was their vow of chastity. Any Vestal Virgin who broke this vow faced whipping to death or burial alive. Apparently only 20 Vestals broke their vows in over a thousand years.

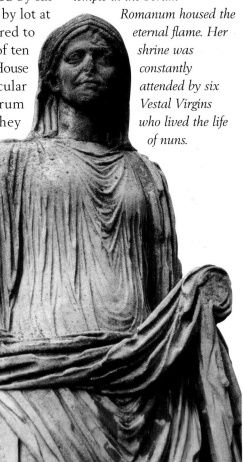

Below: A 3rd-century AD statue of a Vestal Virgin. The Roman goddess of the household hearth, Vesta's temple in the Forum Romanum housed the eternal flame. Her shrine was constantly attended by six Vestal Virgins who lived the life of nuns.

VENUS, VULCAN AND OTHER GODS

The Romans adopted gods and goddesses from many different civilizations. Venus, for example, filled a huge gap in the Roman pantheon, which was notably lacking in amorous or beautiful deities, and Vulcan was identified with the Greek god Hephaestus.

VENUS

Originally a minor Italian nature goddess associated with spring, in the 3rd century BC Venus became identified with Aphrodite, the daughter of Zeus/Jupiter and supremely beautiful Greek goddess of love. Venus had many shrines, including a Greek shrine on Mount Eryx in Sicily and another in Pompeii. Her fame grew when Julius Caesar, claiming divine ancestry for the Julian family, ordered the building of the temple of Venus Genetrix in 46BC.

According to Homer, Aphrodite/Venus was the mother of Aeneas, the Trojan prince. The fragmentary Roman legends that Virgil transformed into the *Aeneid* state that Aeneas had fled burning Troy to found Lavinium, the precursor of Rome. As the Julio-Claudian emperors claimed descent through Aeneas, Venus was linked with Rome's imperial destiny. Hadrian dedicated a huge double temple to Venus and Roma Dea in AD135.

Imperial propaganda did not reduce the allure of the sweet-natured goddess. Born from the sea's foam, she was wafted ashore naked on a shell by gentle zephyrs, to land at Paphos in Cyprus, where the Horae, the attendant hours, were waiting to clothe her and usher her into the presence of the gods. All were overwhelmed by her. Both Mars and Mercury had affairs with her as erotic chaos broke out on Mount Olympus, the gods' home. Finally Juno and Minerva, furiously jealous, competed in a beauty parade with her to see which goddess Paris would pick. The Trojan prince chose Venus and from the other goddesses' undying enmity arose the Trojan war. Aeneas was born of Venus'

Above: Venus by the forge of Vulcan, the blacksmith god to whom the goddess of love was improbably married – although not for long.

Below: The birth of Venus and her passage ashore on a seashell, depicted on a fresco in Pompeii.

affair with the Trojan Anchises, but she herself was no warrior-goddess and relied upon her charms, rather than strength. Doves were sacred to her, as was the evening star, the planet Venus. Lucretius started his great philosophical poem *De rerum natura* (*About the Nature of Things*) with a passionate invocation to Venus: *Aeneadum genetrix, hominum divumque voluptas, alma Venus* ("Mother of Aeneas, delight of gods and men, kindly Venus"). Catullus and other poets constantly invoked her and she remains the most enduringly appealing of all Graeco-Roman deities.

VULCAN

The ugly blacksmith god Vulcan was the polar opposite of the graceful goddess of love. Under the name Volcanus he was an ancient Latin deity, an original protector of Rome and consort of Juno.

After Jupiter displaced him, Vulcan concentrated on working in the hot bowels of the Earth: the Romans placed his divine smithy both inside Mount Etna and on the volcanic Aeolian islands. Vulcan was lamed after being thrown from Mount Olympus for interfering in a quarrel between his parents Jupiter and Juno. Falling into the sea, he was rescued by nymphs and there learnt his metal-working trade, creating a marvellous gold throne that glued Juno to it when she sat down. To obtain her release, the gods had to agree to allow him to marry Venus. Their marriage was not made in heaven, however, for Venus, repelled by the dirty smith, had an affair with Mars. Vulcan angrily threw a metal net over the adulterous couple as they slept, trapping them for the other gods' mirth.

JANUS

One of the very few Roman gods without a Greek counterpart, Janus was an ancient and popular Italic god, his cult traditionally established by Romulus.

Janus was the god of all doorways and public gates through which roads passed. His emblems were his keys and the *virga* (stick) that porters used to drive intruders

away. Janus was most famous for being *Janus bifrons*, two-faced, so that he could see people coming and going. Because he was the god of new beginnings, the first month of the year, January, was named after him, and the first day of each month was sacred to him. In the Forum Romanum his temple had gates that were opened in time of war and – far more rarely – closed in times of peace.

LARES AND PENATES

The domestic gods Lares and Penates, the guardian spirits of the household, were also typically Roman deities. Each Roman house traditionally had one *lar* (the word was originally Etruscan, meaning prince) and two *penates*, whose names derived from *penus*, larder.

The *lar* was invoked on all important family occasions such as marriages and funerals. A bride crossing the threshold of her new household made an offering to the house's *lar*, whose image was always decorated at festival times. There was also a *lar* of the crossroads.

The *penates* oversaw the family supply of food and drink and their altar was the hearth, which they shared with Vesta. On the Ara Pacis, Aeneas is shown sacrificing to the *penates*.

Left: Vulcan's forge, a 2nd-century AD mosaic from Dougga in North Africa. The god of all metal workers, clever but unlovely, Vulcan had his forge either beneath Mt Etna in Sicily or in the Aeolian islands just to the north.

Below: The two-headed god of the crossroads, Janus was unusual in that he was a completely Roman deity. His ancient worship, traditionally started by Romulus, was very popular throughout Italy.

EMPEROR WORSHIP AND THE GODDESS ROMA

Above: Augustus with his toga pulled up over his head to indicate that he is acting as a priest. He took the title Pontifex Maximus (Highest Priest) but never let himself be worshipped as a god in Rome or Italy while he was alive. He was only deified at his death.

Since the reign of Alexander the Great (336–323BC), the Greeks had hailed as gods kings or generals whom they wished to honour or appease. The step from superhuman hero to demi-god or god was a short one in a world filled with gods. When Roman generals succeeded Alexander's successors as arbiters of the eastern Mediterranean, Greeks began treating them, too, as divine, starting with Flaminius in 196BC. Many cities set up altars to the deity Roma Dea, the goddess Rome. Mark Antony, who ruled the East from 42–31BC, was hailed as an avatar of Dionysus/Bacchus in Greek cities in Asia Minor and in Egypt, where he sat enthroned beside Cleopatra dressed as Isis. This did not help his reputation among the Romans, however. Augustus' supporters said that Antony had gone native and lost his Roman *virtus*.

THE IMPERIAL CULT

Augustus dealt pragmatically with the desire of many of his non-Roman subjects to worship him in his turn. He allowed altars or temples to his *genius* (guardian spirit) or *numen* (divinity) to be erected across the provinces. In Aphrodisias in southern Asia Minor, a large *Sebasteion* (temple to Augustus) was built by prominent local individuals and served by priests recruited from local aristocrats. Cities competed with each other to offer the emperor honours and sacred hymns were composed to him at Pergamum. More deliberately, Augustus built a small temple on the Athenian acropolis to Augustus and the goddess Roma combined, underlining Rome's divinely sanctioned power in the heart of Greece.

In Egypt, where Augustus was the heir to the divine pharaohs and Ptolemies, his worship presented no problems. At the other end of the empire in Gaul, a Great Altar to Augustus and Roma was set up at Lyons (Lugdunum), Gaul's largest city. Representatives of the three Gallic provinces came every year to demonstrate their devotion to Rome and the emperor. Many Romanized Gallic nobles happily contributed to such cults, which demonstrated their new status in the empire. At Colchester (Camulodunum) in the new province of Britain, a temple to Claudius the god was established but proved less popular. It was burnt down in Boudicca's revolt of AD60. However, this reaction was uncommon.

In contrast, the Roman nobility, whose support Augustus needed to run the empire, regarded any presumption of divinity by the emperor as an outrage tantamount to tyranny, and he had to tread carefully. During his lifetime, Augustus was still only *princeps* (first citizen). Although he prominently advertised himself as *divi filius*, son of a god, he never allowed anyone to call him a god in Rome or to build a temple to him in Italy.

It was different with the dead, however. Julius Caesar was deified posthumously and a temple was built to him. On his death Augustus was also declared a god by the Senate, his soul soaring into heaven in the form of an eagle released from his burning pyre. Most popular emperors were subsequently deified, although rulers found odious by the Senate – Tiberius, Caligula, Nero, Domitian, Commodus – were denied this honour. Antoninus Pius (ruled AD138–61) had to threaten to abdicate before the Senate would deify Hadrian, a superb ruler but one who had not got on with the Senate. Later Septimius Severus deified the megalomaniac Commodus to link his family with the Antonines.

Wiser emperors – Augustus, Trajan, Marcus Aurelius – accepted these encomia reluctantly, but by the 3rd century emperors were assuming divine attributes during their lifetime and some, especially those who had inherited the throne, let this worship go their heads. Caligula (ruled AD37–41) was one of the maddest, addressing Jupiter's statue on the Capitoline as an equal. Nero saw himself as an incarnation of the sungod Helios, and Domitian insisted on being called *dominus et deus* (Lord and God). Commodus even wanted to rename Rome after himself. However, most educated people knew that the emperor was not literally divine and throwing incense on the altar to the emperor and Roma required no religious commitment. It was merely indicative of a general patriotic loyalty.

PERSECUTION

Not all the peoples of the empire could accept this, however. The Jews, spread around the Mediterranean even before Titus destroyed the Temple in Jerusalem in AD70, regarded emperor worship as an abomination. The Romans respected the Jewish religion for its antiquity and dignity (although they found it puzzling) and exempted Jews from emperor worship. When Caligula tried to have his statue installed in the Holy of Holies in the temple in Jerusalem, he almost triggered an uprising, but this was an exception.

The Christians, who were recognized as a sect distinct from the Jews by AD64, were not exempted in the same way and so were intermittently persecuted. However, as the correspondence between the emperor Trajan and Pliny the Younger, governor of Bithynia, reveals, the Romans did not usually seek out Christians to persecute. It was only during the crises of the 3rd century AD, when Rome's rulers appealed to every god in heaven to aid the stricken empire, that Christians were harshly persecuted for risking the gods' wrath. Even then, only the most stubborn – or devout – experienced martyrdom.

Above: Base of the Column of Antoninus Pius (AD138–61), showing the apotheosis of Faustina, his wife, and also of himself.

Above: Gold coin showing the head of the deified Claudius. Even the undignified Claudius was worshipped in Britain during his lifetime and became a god after his death.

BACCHUS AND CYBELE

The official Roman gods were vital to the maintenance of Rome's political fortunes and of family life. However, they lacked the mystical appeal of the new gods and mystery cults from the East which promised immortality to those initiated into their secret rites. The Senate, alarmed that secret devotions might lead adherents to neglect their social and political duties, initially tried to restrict them.

BACCHUS

The Romans had their own cheerful rustic wine god, Liber Pater, whose festival they celebrated in March. However, Bacchus, identified with the Greek Dionysus, the most dangerous god in the Greek pantheon, was very different.

Born to Semele, a Theban princess, son of Jupiter, the young Bacchus overcame the jealous goddess Juno's varied attempts to kill him. (His mother was blasted by lightning and he himself was chopped up by Titans and cooked in a cauldron.)

Resurrected by Jupiter, Bacchus was educated partly by nymphs and led a procession of satyrs, muses and maenads in a chariot drawn by tigers or panthers. He was famed for spreading the cult of wine and his intoxicated festivals.

Bacchus married the abandoned Cretan princess Ariadne on Naxos and drove the mother of King Pentheus of Thebes (who had imprisoned him) so mad that she blindly tore her son to pieces. In classical Greece, Bacchus as Dionysus was recognized as the official god of drama. His spring festival was noted both for the plays staged under his auspices and for the ecstatic excesses of the maenads, his female followers.

Later, Bacchus' cult spread wider and became secretive. In 186BC the Roman Senate ordered the suppression of most altars to the god throughout Italy after the "Bacchanalian incident", details of which remain obscure. The cult, which had entered Rome via the Greek cities of southern Italy, went underground for a time until, wiser than King Pentheus, the Romans accepted Bacchus' worship.

The remarkable murals of the Villa of Mysteries at Pompeii show a woman being whipped and then comforted while a winged *daemon* (spirit) looks on. The murals probably depict an initiation scene from this mysterious cult, which was especially popular with women.

CYBELE, THE *MAGNA MATER*

Few cults less suited to the dignified Roman Republic could be imagined than the orgiastic worship of Cybele, the *Magna Mater* (Great Mother). A Phrygian fertility goddess, she was worshipped on mountain tops and underground. Her son Attis emasculated himself in ecstatic devotion to her in an act her followers repeated in public in gory rituals. All her priests were eunuchs, something no

Above: Bacchantes dancing with a whip and cymbals from the House of the Mysteries, Pompeii.

Below: The so-called Temple of Bacchus (Dionysus), the god of wine and ecstasy, at Baalbek, Lebanon.

Roman citizen could be and retain his citizenship. However, in the darkest days of the war against Hannibal, the Romans consulted the Sibylline Books. These predicted that Italy would only be freed if the "Idaean mother of Pessinus" was brought to Rome. The Romans understood this to refer to Cybele and set about bringing her cult to Rome. It arrived in the form of a black stone, possibly a meteorite, in 204BC, just as Hannibal was about to leave Italy.

Installed in 191BC in her own temple on the Palatine, the *Magna Mater* had a special band of eunuch priests (*galli*) to serve her, and her festival, the Megalensia, was held annually from the 5th to 10th April, with religious processions, games and theatrical performances in the Circus Maximus. Although a Roman magistrate presided over the ceremonies, the *galli*, dressed in bright-coloured robes stained with blood from their self-flagellation, offended Roman sensibilities, for Roman citizens were forbidden to be priests. Finally the open-minded emperor Claudius (ruled AD41–54) incorporated her cult into the official Roman pantheon.

THE PYTHAGOREANS

Pythagoras (*c.* 570–500BC) was the great mystic among mathematicians. One of the leading early Greek Presocratic philosophers, traditionally he was the first man to call himself a philosopher.

Little definite is known about Pythagoras' life or teaching, but he reputedly believed in metempsychosis, the transmigration of souls, whereby human souls are reincarnated in animals or plants according to their past lives. He also advocated strict vegetarianism and forbade the eating of beans because they caused the breaking of wind, which he held to contain the human soul.

Pythagoras moved from his native island of Samos to southern Italy, where he established a school at Crotona. There he taught a select few mathematics, astronomy and music. He also taught a secret political programme that allowed

the Pythagoreans to wield real power for some years in several western Greek cities before they were eventually expelled and driven underground.

Under the Romans their beliefs revived. Nigidius Figulus, a praetor in 58BC, was a Neopythagorean as, apparently, was Apollonius of Tyana *c.* AD200. A tiny underground basilica by the Porta Maggiore in Rome, discovered by chance in 1917 and decorated with exquisite mythological scenes about the love and death of the Greek poet Sappho, is probably Neopythagorean. The cult clearly had to remain half-secret, however. One likely member, Statilius Taurus, was condemned in AD53 for practising "magic arts". In fact the Neopythagoreans were the most intellectual of the mystery cults.

Right: A eunuch priest of Cybele, the Great Mother goddess. Her worship was imported into Rome in 204BC.

Above: A 3rd-century AD mosaic showing the triumph of Bacchus over the Indians in his tiger-drawn chariot. The Romans adopted the worship and myths of Dionysus, the Greek god of drama, whom they called Bacchus.

NEW GODS FROM THE EAST

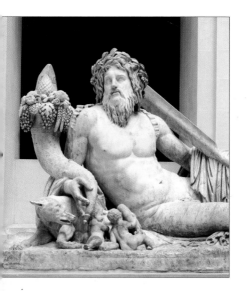

Above: Statue of Tiber, the god of the river. It was found at the sanctuary of Isis and Sarapis in the Campus Martius, where Caligula had built a temple to the two Egyptian deities.

Below: A 2nd-century AD relief from Alexandria in Egypt showing the bearded Sarapis seated between the goddesses Demeter and Venus (Aphrodite). His worship was more usually associated with that of Isis.

For the Romans as for the Greeks, the traditional gods of pharaonic Egypt, such as the jackal-headed Anubis, seemed absurdly zoomorphic, suited only for Egyptian peasants. Nonetheless, the antiquity and mystery of the land impressed Western rulers from Alexander the Great on and two deities emerged from Egypt that spread around the Roman empire as far north-west as Britain: Isis and Sarapis.

ISIS

The greatest goddess of Egypt in Hellenistic and Roman times, Isis was of great antiquity. Originally she had been simply a local goddess of the Delta. According to much-embroidered myth, she was the consort and sister of Osiris and mother of the hawk god Horus. When Set, their evil brother, murdered Osiris, she wandered the earth to find her husband's dismembered body, mourning as she went. The legend reveals that she was originally a fertility goddess connected with the natural cycle of death and rebirth, like Cybele and many other goddesses. Under the Greek-speaking Ptolemies, who ruled Egypt 323–30BC,

she was Hellenized and her role expanded into that of a cosmic saviour. Aspects of her cult then acquired genuine spiritual and ethical elements that Apuleius later voiced most lyrically in his novel *The Golden Ass* of *c.* AD150.

As her worship spread around the Mediterranean from its origins in Alexandria, Isis became known as Stella Maris (Star of the Sea), the divine protector of sailors and fishermen. In Rome, spectacular annual festivals in her honour celebrated the start of the sailing season on 5th March with *navigium Isidis* (the Relapse of the Ship) and its completion in the autumn.

Isis' strongest appeal initially was to women, freedmen and slaves; old-fashioned Romans such as Augustus and Tiberius disapproved of her. The emperor Caligula (ruled AD37–41) was a devotee, however, and encouraged the building of a temple to her and her co-Egyptian deity Sarapis in the Campus Martius in Rome. Pompeii boasted a fine temple of Isis, the earliest one in Italy, as did many other cities across the empire, especially those involved with foreign trade such as Ostia. These temples had heavily Egyptian decorations to stress their exotic appeal, but the cult itself seems to have been uplifting rather than orgiastic. A mural from Herculaneum shows very solemn-looking priests and worshippers conducting ceremonies. In the final section of *The Golden Ass*, Apuleius waxed lyrical about how Isis appeared to him in a dream, saying "I am the first of heavenly beings, mother of the gods, I am Minerva, Venus, Diana…the Universal Mother, mistress of the elements, primeval child of time…queen of the dead, queen also of the immortals".

The worship of Isis continued to grow through the 3rd century and even survived early Christian persecutions; her great temple at Philae in Egypt was only

Right: The worship of Isis, the great goddess of Egypt, was very popular. The rites were dignified if mysterious, as this fresco from Herculaneum shows.

finally closed in the 6th century. Some aspects of her cult, including her blue robe and the title Stella Maris, were taken over by the cult of the Virgin Mary.

SARAPIS

Sarapis was a wholly syncretic deity, invented under the Ptolemies who conflated Osiris, Isis' consort, with the sacred Apis bulls. The resulting god, Osor-apis, or Sarapis, then became identified with the dynasty and with Zeus/Jupiter.

Worshipped in Alexandria as a bearded man, Sarapis was seen by the Greeks as a healing god, similar to Asclepius, the Greek healing god who was introduced to Rome in 291BC. Sick people went to his temple to be cured through divine dreams in a process called incubation.

Meanwhile, and supposedly connected with this but in reality perpetuating a far older cult, Egyptian priests continued to worship Apis at Memphis.

Vespasian (ruled AD69–79) titled himself the new Sarapis when he launched his victorious bid for the imperial throne in Alexandria in AD69. Later Caracalla (ruled AD211–17) built an impressive Serapeum on the Quirinal Hill in Rome.

THE SIBYL

At several desperate moments in its history, the Sibyl and the Sibylline books were of crucial importance to Rome. Traditionally, the Sibyl, a priestess of Apollo from Cumae, a Greek colony near Naples, offered to sell King Tarquin nine books of prophecy in the 6th century BC. King Tarquin refused twice to buy them, baulking at the price. Each time he refused, the priestess threw three of the books into the fire and doubled the price of the remainder. Tarquin eventually capitulated and bought the last three, which were then kept in the Capitol. The books were consulted by the Senate in emergencies about which foreign gods to import. An outbreak of plague led to the introduction of the worship of Apollo in 431BC. The books were also thought to contain prophecies and some Christians later maintained that they foretold the birth of Christ. They were all lost in the invasions of the 5th century AD.

Right: A wayfarer consults the Sibyl. Originally a priestess of Apollo from Greek Cumae, she became central to Rome's religious practices.

CULT OF THE SUN

Above: The 3rd-century AD Altar to Mithras in the mithraeum of the Circus Maximus in Rome. Most shrines to this god were underground, like this one. Only the initiated were able to watch the rites whose secrets are now lost.

The Graeco-Roman pantheon was essentially anthropomorphic and did not deify natural phenomena. However, the Greeks worshipped the sun god Helios just as the Romans worshipped Sol Indiges. Worship of Sol Invictus, the Unconquered Sun, was at times linked to the worship of Mithras.

MITHRAS

Possibly Indo-Iranian in origin, Mithras became an archetypal saviour deity for the Romans, a precursor and rival to Christianity. First appearing in Rome in the 1st century BC, Mithras was usually portrayed in Persian clothes wearing a Phrygian cap (from Asia Minor), killing the bull of cosmic darkness.

There were strong astrological associations to the cult of Mithras. Aion (impersonal time) sometimes appeared as a lion-headed deity beside him on carvings and the evil scorpion was depicted being crushed. Mithras offered his worshippers redemption from the otherwise inexorable fate revealed by astrology.

Mithraism's hierarchy mirrored that of the Roman army, of which most of its adherents were members, and initiation into his worship came in grades. Each congregation was composed of *fratres* (brothers) and *patres* (fathers) – titles the Christians later copied – who promised to support each other.

The final initiation rite may have required the neophyte to lie in a pit while the blood of a freshly sacrificed bull showered down on him but, as with other mystery rites, the exact details of Mithraic rites are unknown. The cult was spread around the empire mainly by the army, but it also appealed to unmilitary types such as merchants of Ostia, where 15 *mithraea* (shrines) have been found, and to the emperor Nero. Ever interested in novelties, Nero appeared dressed as Mithras when investing Tiridates as king of Armenia in a grand ceremony at Rome in AD66. In the 2nd century AD, Hadrian and Commodus were initiated as emperors and so, reputedly, was Julian,

Right: One of the most attractive aspects of Mithraism was its practice of mutual support, which rivalled Christianity's. Here a mystical banquet sanctifies the solidarity of his worshippers.

the last pagan emperor (ruled AD361–3) who ordered the building of a *mithraeum* in Constantinople, the new capital. There was an underground *mithraeum* in London, whose ruins are almost the only Roman buildings which survive in the open in the city. An obvious limitation to the spread of Mithraism was its restriction to men. Mithras' cult vanished with the fall of the Western empire in the 5th century AD.

THE UNCONQUERED SUN

During the imperial period there was a growing tendency among the intellectual to look for a unifying divine force behind the empire's plethora of deities. This is implied in the dedication of the emperor Hadrian's greatest temple, the Pantheon, to *all* the gods.

Sol Invictus, the Unconquered Sun, was first mentioned in the 2nd century AD and the emperor Septimius Severus added a radiant solar nimbus to his imperial attributes around the same time. His son Caracalla, who extended Roman citizenship to (almost) all free inhabitants of the empire in AD212, unwittingly furthered such syncretic attempts to unite the gods in the *pax deorum*, the harmony of the heavens. (Caracalla was concerned chiefly with extending the death duties which were paid only by Roman citizens.)

The solar cult took a giant step forward in the reign of Elagabus (ruled AD218–22), the juvenile high priest of the sun god Baal in Emesa. His orgiastic worship of his Syrian deity, aimed at making Baal superior to all Rome's gods and said to involve human sacrifices and mass homosexual orgies, proved too much for Romans. After his assassination his successor Alexander Severus carefully restored the older gods.

Alexander reputedly had images of many saviours in his private chapel, including Orpheus, the legendary poet, Apollonius of Tyana, a recent pagan magus, Abraham and Christ. Yet in the subsequent catastrophic decades, when the empire almost foundered amid endless civil wars, barbarian invasions and

Above: A reconstruction of a Mithraic temple showing Mithras slaying the bull of cosmic darkness. The most popular saviour god among the legions, Mithras was also worshipped by civilians, but his cult excluded women.

massive economic disruption, people yearned for a simpler, universal god. Among these, Sol Invictus, immediately visible as an object of adoration and the obvious bringer of light to all men, incorruptible and perfectly round, had the strongest appeal. The emperor Aurelian (ruled AD270–5), who regained Gaul and the Eastern provinces for the empire and built Rome's new walls, also built a fine circular temple to Sol Invictus in Rome. With a special new priestly college, Sol Invictus was now made the primary object of official imperial worship in Rome and across the empire and 25th December, the dedication day of the temple, was made a public holiday. Christmas was later deliberately moved to that date.

The tetrarch Constantius Chlorus (ruled AD293–306) also worshipped the Unconquered Sun as did Constantine I in his early years, until the Edict of Milan in AD313, when he and his co-emperor Licinius proclaimed tolerance for all religions. Even in AD324, after his final victory over Licinius, Constantine was still issuing coins bearing images of Sol Invictus and in Constantinople he erected a statue of himself with a crown of solar rays. Although this reflected political caution vis-à-vis his overwhelmingly pagan subjects, it also shows the solar cult was not just an imperial preference.

Below: Head of the sun-god Helios or Sol Invictus. The Romans were slow to worship the impersonal sun, but 3rd-century AD crises led Aurelian to institute an official cult of the sun to help unite the empire.

CHRISTIANITY: TRIBULATION TO TRIUMPH

Above: A head of Constantine I hints at the colossal arrogance of the first emperor to actively promote Christianity.

Below: The Apostles Peter and Paul from an early 4th-century AD Roman bas-relief. St Peter's, Rome, was one of the first great basilicas.

In *c.* AD33 Jesus, an obscure but probably heterodox Jewish preacher, was put to death on the reluctant orders of the governor of Judaea, Pontius Pilate. The event had no impact on the Roman empire, although Jesus' followers claimed to have seen him alive soon after and began preaching his resurrection, first to Jewish communities around the Mediterranean and then, under the forceful guidance of Paul of Tarsus, to the wider Greek and Latin-speaking world.

A NEW RELIGION

Initially considered a form of Judaism by the Romans, Christianity was recognized as a distinct sect in AD64 after the great fire of Rome, which the people blamed Nero for starting. The Christians made useful scapegoats for the emperor, who had some rounded up, coated with pitch and set alight. Even Roman audiences

found this hard to stomach and such mass persecutions were long the exception. The Christians were not popular, however. Tacitus, writing *c.* AD100, called them "haters of the human race". Like many Romans he misunderstood Christianity's doctrines and saw the eucharist as an orgy involving cannibalism.

Christianity first appealed mainly to women and slaves and so attracted official suspicion. However, letters between Trajan and Pliny the Younger, *c.* AD110, show the emperor restraining would-be persecutors, insisting that Christians be given fair trials and forbidding anonymous letters of accusation. Hadrian restated this approach in AD122.

Although mobs seem to have enjoyed tormenting this helpless minority, Christianity continued to expand and the Christian church's cellular structure proved supportive in a way unmatched by any other cult. Christianity also appealed to intellectuals (such as St Clement) and to the illiterate alike.

What Christians believed did not worry most pagans; it was what they openly refused to accept that caused problems, especially when the empire was in crisis. By refusing even to sacrifice incense to Roma and the imperial *genius* (spirit), Christians were offending the *pax deorum*, the gods' united protection that the empire desperately needed. This led to imperially sponsored persecutions, from the brief attack under Decius (AD251) to the Great Persecution launched by Diocletian and Galerius in AD303.

Not only priests but ordinary believers were now hunted out. Diocletian himself was no fanatic – he had a Christian wife – nor were many of his officials. Transcripts of AD303 show the governor of Egypt urging his Christian prisoners to reconsider their decision the next day. Many Christians did abjure, but Christian *martyrs* (witnesses) went to their deaths with impressive confidence in the life to come, finally convincing Galerius and many others that persecution was pointless. In AD311 Galerius rescinded his edicts and asked Christians, too, to pray for the empire.

CONSTANTINE'S CONVERSION

Traditionally Constantine had a dream the night before his victory at the Milvian Bridge in AD312 which led him to put Christian insignia on his army's standards, so guaranteeing him victory. Afterwards, he noticeably failed to climb the Capitol to make the usual offerings to Jupiter.

While the Edict of Milan in AD313 granted toleration to all religions, Constantine attended the Council of Bishops at Arles in AD314 and the more important Council of Nicaea in AD325. At both, he vainly strove to reconcile warring factions, for Christians, upon ceasing to be persecuted themselves, now began persecuting each other.

Further victories confirmed Constantine in his belief that he was protected by the Christian god. However, he continued to employ pagans and for a time himself observed pagan rituals, even permitting the restoration of old temples in Byzantium after he made it his capital.

Such moves were common sense, as perhaps 95 per cent of his court, army and empire were non-Christian. Nonetheless, he tried to restrict public pagan sacrifices and exempted the Christian clergy from onerous public duties where possible

Constantine also had material reasons for favouring Christianity. The pagan temples whose despoliation he started were filled not just with centuries of great artworks, many covered with gold and ivory, but had also been used as safe deposits by locals in the absence of reliable banks. Constantine's looting of old treasures – comparable in scale perhaps to Henry VIII's dissolution of the monasteries – helped to pay for his huge building programme. This included not only his

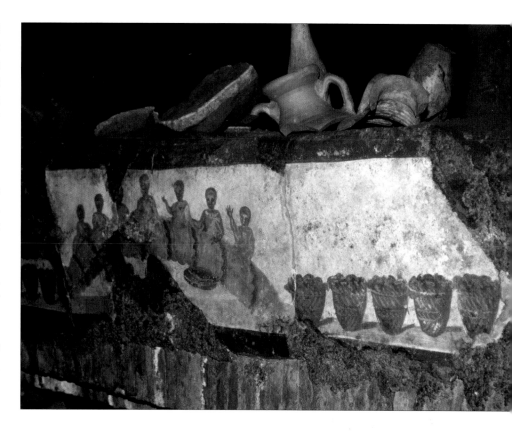

many secular works – in Rome and Constantinople – but also vast numbers of churches, including Old St Peter's and St John Lateran in Rome.

When Constantine died in AD337 (he was buried in the Church of the Apostles in Constantinople), his successors continued his Christianizing policies. The notable but brief exception of Julian's two-year reign revived pagan hopes but failed to shake the slowly emerging Christian establishment.

Imperial toleration of paganism, which was always reluctant, vanished in the later 4th century AD. In AD386 the fervently Christian emperor Theodosius I ordered the removal of the statue of the goddess Victory from the Senate House in Rome, despite the impassioned protestations of Symmachus, a pagan, that "So great a mystery could not be approached by one path alone".

With the disasters of the 5th century AD, most Romans in the West turned in despair to Christianity, whose kingdom was not of this world. However, in the East paganism survived in substantial pockets into the 6th century AD.

Above: The disciples pictured in the catacombs of St Callistus in Rome. Christians may have worshipped in the catacombs and were buried there, but they did not live there.

Below: This mosaic from the 5th-century AD Mausoleum of Galla Placidia in Ravenna shows St Lawrence the Martyr as a deacon carrying a cross. Martyrs were much revered.

SPORT AND GAMES

Games, especially gladiatorial combats and chariot races, are among the most famous, even notorious, aspects of life in ancient Rome. Many Roman cities built amphitheatres. The Colosseum in Rome was the largest such arena in the Roman world, but gladiatorial games were first staged in the Forum Romanum and beast displays in the Circus Maximus, which could accommodate possibly six times as many spectators as the Colosseum.

The games required expensively trained professionals, most of whom were slaves, and did not necessarily involve the killing of the human combatants. Although the chariot races staged in the Circus Maximus in Rome were indisputably expensive and dangerous, the arenas of less well-developed provinces such as Britain may have seen far more sporting contests and military tattoos than gladiator fights.

The Circus and the Colosseum were also the venues for *venationes*, wild beast hunts and games which, along with public executions, were much relished by audiences. Roman theatre, in contrast, saw mimes, dances and the Roman *pantomimus* – an entertainment which often involved real violence – grow in popularity during the empire.

Physical fitness was long thought desirable in Rome, where men were liable for arduous military service in the Republic. Exercise grounds were later laid out in Rome and other cities.

Left: A wild beast hunt in a 4th-century AD mosaic.
These venationes *(wild beast hunts) rivalled gladiatorial displays in their popularity.*

GLADIATORIAL COMBATS

Above: A terracotta oil lamp from the 1st century AD, showing gladiators in combat. Gladiatorial combats were popular decorative themes.

Below: A Retiarius (right) and a Secutor (left) depicted on a mosaic from a Roman villa in Negra de Valpolicella, Italy.

Gladiatorial combats were funerary in origin, hence their name *numera* (rewards, sacrifices). The spirits of the dead were thought to appreciate human blood, so captives or slaves were set to fight each other to death at aristocratic funerals.

The first recorded gladiatorial show in Rome was staged in 264 BC, when three pairs of gladiators fought to the death in the Forum Boarium (Cattle Market) for the funeral of Marcus Iunius Brutus. Over the next 200 years, Roman nobles competed to put on ever more lavish shows. In 65 BC, Julius Caesar displayed 250 pairs of gladiators at funeral games for his father – who had died 20 years before.

This extravagance, which the Senate tried to limit, was an attempt to win votes, for, as Juvenal later noted, *duas tantem res anxius optat,/ panem et circenses* ("The mob cares only for bread and circuses"). Finally the emperor became the main, often sole, provider of games for Rome's frequent public holidays, while in other cities local magnates continued to provide gorily expensive games involving gladiators and wild animals. Games were often staged as part of ceremonies to do with the imperial cult in the provinces or with triumphs in Rome under the emperors.

At first, gladiators were recruited from among slaves, condemned criminals or war captives. Later, as supplies of these groups dwindled, some free men volunteered for a fixed, usually three- or five-year term. Some slaves were sold off for training as gladiators by owners who wanted to punish them, until Hadrian forbade the practice in the 2nd century AD.

A successful gladiator might hope to earn his *rudis* (wooden sword) of liberty, after three years in the arena and to make enough money from gifts to retire in comfort before he was killed.

SCHOOLS FOR GLADIATORS

Gladiatorial training was always arduous and often brutal. Petronius recorded the oath of obedience that the *tiro* (novice gladiator) swore to his *lanista* (trainer), "We solemnly swear to obey the *lanista* in everything. To endure burning, imprisonment, flogging and even death by the sword". Although discipline was savage, the food was good and accommodation not bad by contemporary standards.

Novice gladiators learned how to fight with wooden swords and wicker shields, feinting at the *palus* (wooden post) before progressing to real but padded weapons in a way that paralleled military training. *Lanistae* were used in the later 2nd century BC to train soldiers and in emergencies, such as the Marcomanni invasions of AD 167, gladiators could be enrolled into the army, receiving their freedom in return. As it took several years to train a skilled gladiator, they did not usually fight to the death.

Training schools for gladiators were established across Italy and then the Western parts of the empire. In Rome, about 2,000 gladiators, along with doctors, armourers and trainers, lived in one of four *ludi* (schools), of which the biggest was the Ludus Magnus, located just 60 yards east of the Colosseum. Probably started under Domitian (ruled AD81–96), its construction was completed under Hadrian 30 years later. It was an imposing building of brick-faced concrete with a central courtyard surrounded by porticoes. Occupying much of this courtyard was an arena large enough to accommodate 3,000 spectators, where gladiators practised. The Ludus Magnus was connected with the Colosseum by an underground tunnel.

To the south of the Ludus Magnus and much the same size was the Ludus Matutinus, where *venatores*, wild beast fighters, were trained. These schools were considered so central to Rome's well-being that they were eventually run by the state. The emperors appointed Praetorian Prefects to recruit and supervise the training of new gladiators.

TYPES OF GLADIATOR

By the early imperial period there were a number of different types of gladiator, who were usually identified by their equipment and fighting tactics.

The Samnite or *hoplomachus* was originally a light-armed fighter, who was not necessarily a Samnite but who fought like one. He became progressively more heavily armed and armoured until he was called a *hoplomachus*, like a Greek heavy infantryman. He now wore a large-crested helmet with thigh-length greaves and carried a large rectangular shield and a stabbing sword (the *gladius hispaniensis*), much like a legionary.

The Thracian gladiator emerged in the 2nd century BC when Rome first encountered this warlike part of the Balkans. He was armed with a small round or square shield and two thigh-length greaves and carried a *sica*, a typical curved weapon from the Danube.

The Gaul was at first lightly armed, with a long flat shield and a cut and thrust sword about 2ft (60cm) long. By the end of the Republic he too had gained a helmet and a slashing sword. He then became better known as a *murmillo*, from the Greek fish *murmillon* which adorned his helmet.

The Secutor, the traditional opponent of the net-wielding Retiarius (literally sword man), was among the most recognizable of gladiators, for he had a unique egg-shaped helmet with a metal crest but no brim. He bore the legionary's *scutum* (rectangular shield) and stabbing sword and had a laminated *manicae* (arm-guard).

The Retiarius was armed with a *rete* (net) and trident and had defensive armour only on his left arm and shoulder. He normally fought one of the more heavily-armed gladiators. Technically, the Retiarius was not a gladiator since he did not have a sword.

There are records of women gladiators, who fought each other and wild beasts, but they were less common and in AD200 were banned altogether.

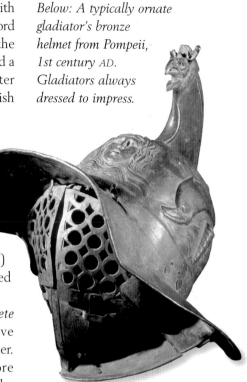

Below: A typically ornate gladiator's bronze helmet from Pompeii, 1st century AD. Gladiators always dressed to impress.

Below: This swordsman, probably a hoplomachos *or* murmillo, *seems to have just finished off a Retiarius, a trident-wielding netman, who is lying beside him.*

THE GREAT GAMES

Above: Gladiatorial combats continued into the 4th century AD, as this mosaic shows. Here a heavily armoured gladiator is shown with a dead Retiarius.

By the time of the late Republic and early empire huge numbers of gladiators were assembled and wounded or killed for special celebrations. For example, the games that marked the inauguration of the Amphitheatrum Flavium, or Colosseum, in AD80, reputedly lasted 100 days.

THE CONDUCT OF THE GAMES

Such games opened with a procession of gladiators, who had had a special dinner (the *libera cena*) in public the night before, although not all may have been feeling hungry. To rousing music from a band in the arena – consisting typically of a water organ, horn blowers and trumpeters – they marched around the arena two abreast in full costume, with purple and gold embroideries if they could afford it. When they reached the *pulvinar* (imperial box), they raised their right hands and cried out, *Ave, Caesar! Morituri te salutant!* ("Hail Caesar, those about to die salute you!")

The gladiators were then paired off by lot. Different types of gladiator were pitted against each other; a nimble Retiarius against a heavier Secutor, for example. Often the *lanista* was present less as a

Below: Terracotta figurines showing two gladiators fighting. Both are similarly armed with swords.

referee than to goad them on with whips and cries of *Iugula! Verbera!* ("Kill! Strike!"), cries which the crowd echoed. Bets were placed and the fight lasted until one combatant was either badly wounded or surrendered. Then trumpets sounded and the wounded man appealed for *missio* (reprieve). The games' sponsor – in Rome normally the emperor – then turned to the spectators. If they thought the gladiator had fought well, they cried *Mitte* ("Let him go"). If the emperor agreed, he would "press his thumb" – a Latin phrase whose precise meaning is unknown but which is interpreted in Hollywood films as raising his thumb. Otherwise, an attendant dressed as Charon, a figure from the underworld, approached with a mallet to finish off the defeated gladiator, whose corpse was dragged through the Porta Libitina (Gate of Execution) with hooks.

The bloodied sand was then replaced while the victor pranced around the arena receiving gifts from spectators and perhaps the palm of success. More rarely he won the wooden foil of freedom. Graffiti from Pompeii, which had the earliest permanent amphitheatre, record various gladiators' fates: "Pugnax, a Thracian of the Neronian *ludus* with three fights to his credit, victorious; Murrans, a *murmillo* of the Neronian *ludus* with three fights to his credit, killed… Atticus, a Thracian with 14 fights, killed".

STAGED SEA BATTLES

Sea fights with small galleys (*naumachiae*) were also staged. At his triumph in 46BC, Julius Caesar had an artificial lake dug in the Campus Martius (just outside the city) and a battle enacted. These battles were very realistic. Galleys were propelled by slaves who fought ferociously. Augustus had a special *naumachia* or artificial lake dug in Trastevere across the Tiber, with its own aqueduct. Here in 2BC he staged a lavish re-enactment of Athens' great victory over the Persians at Salamis in 480BC.

For the inauguration of the works to drain Lake Fucinus under Claudius, a *naumachia* involving 19,000 men took place on the lake. It almost ended in farce when Claudius returned the traditional gladiators' salute, "Hail Caesar, those about to die salute you!" with the quip, "Or not, as the case may be". This so annoyed the gladiators that they downed swords and had to be coaxed back to fight. Nero used Augustus' *naumachia* for varied nocturnal frolics but after that it seems to have fallen into decay. The Colosseum may have been partly flooded for *naumachiae* later.

Most Romans accepted and some even defended gladiatorial shows. Cicero asserted they taught Roman audiences contempt for pain and death, while Pliny the Younger maintained that watching such massacres, in which even criminals and slaves showed a love of glory, would make Romans courageous.

A few emperors, such as Marcus Aurelius, who openly dealt with his correspondence in the arena rather than watching the games, tried to interest the Roman populace in *lusiones*, mock games without bloodshed, but were unsuccessful. Claudius, who watched the fights eagerly and spared no wounded Retiarius, was more typically Roman. Expense led to the decline of the games after the 3rd century AD.

SPARTACUS THE REBEL

The most famous gladiator of them all, who challenged and threatened to overthrow Roman power, Spartacus took his name from the Greek city of Sparta, although he probably came from Thrace. Trained at the Capua *ludus*, he started his revolt there in 73BC, leading the gladiators out from their barracks, then freeing agricultural slaves to form an army many

thousands strong. Reputedly, Spartacus had once served as a Roman soldier, which explains how he managed to defeat hastily conscripted armies sent against him.

For a time Spartacus controlled much of southern Italy. Finally Crassus, the richest man in Rome, was given command. Decimating his legions (killing one man in ten) to restore order, and with the help of Pompey arriving belatedly from Spain, he cornered and destroyed Spartacus' army in 71BC. Along the Via Appia from Rome to Capua 7,000 rebels were crucified in ghastly but effective warning. There were no more such revolts.

Above: An orchestra, sometimes with a woman playing the water organ, often accompanied the games, as in this mosaic from Zliten, near Lepcis Magna, Africa.

Below: In this 4th-century AD mosaic, found on the Via Appia, just outside Rome, gladiatorial combat is carefully controlled by the lanistae, *the trainers. Strict rules governed most combats.*

WILD BEAST GAMES

Above: A bestiarius (animal fighter) is thrown into the air by a bull in this 3rd-century AD funerary stone from Africa. Fighting wild beasts could be very dangerous.

Below: A lion fight in the Circus Maximus in Rome in the 1st century AD. The lion on the right seems to have already killed a man, but is about to be speared himself. On the left a lioness leaps to savage an armed man.

Parallel to the gladiators' fights were the *venationes*, the wild beast games, which were if anything an even larger business. The *venatores* (huntsmen) and the *bestiarii* (animal fighters) had their own *ludus*, the Ludus Matutinus (so-called because the beast displays were usually staged in the morning), although they never enjoyed the same prestige as gladiators.

Venationes provided the Roman urban populace with a glimpse of the often dangerous hunting – for wild boar among other animals – that the emperor himself enjoyed in the country proper. However, they became almost as ruinously expensive as the *munera*.

The first *venationes* or hunting displays started innocuously enough: a hundred elephants that had been captured from the Carthaginians in 251BC were forced to perform tricks. However, in the 2nd century BC more violent displays developed. By 99BC, full-scale fights between elephants were being staged in the Circus Maximus. Marcus Scaurus, who reportedly built a luxurious if temporary amphitheatre of marble and glass in 58BC, imported 150 leopards along with a hippopotamus and five crocodiles for his games. Increasingly bloody *venationes* were hosted from then on.

Caesar had 600 lions, 400 other great cats and 20 elephants in his triumphant *venatio*. Titus surpassed this, killing 5,000 animals on one day to inaugurate the Colosseum in AD80. Trajan had 2,246 wild beasts slaughtered in just one of his many *munera*. The poet Martial mentions more innocent circus turns, including teams of panthers obediently drawing chariots and elephants kneeling to trace Latin phrases in the sand with their trunks. The populace wanted blood, however, and to satisfy it the Romans pitted bears against water buffalos, panthers against leopards, lions against tigers and bulls against rhinoceroses. (The latter were normally victorious, tossing great bulls into the air like balls.)

The *venatores*, armed with spears, bows, daggers and firebrands and sometimes assisted by hunting dogs, fought animals in the arena. Trees and shrubs were placed in the arena to create the illusion of a forest in which the *venatores* hunted and killed the doomed animals. The Romans were no more sentimental about killing animals than about killing humans and viewed the *venationes* as a re-affirmation of their dominance over nature.

Criminals were sometimes executed by the *damnatio ad bestias* (thrown unarmed or with rudimentary weapons into the arena to face wild animals or gladiators). War captives were another source of arena fodder. Under Claudius, captive Britons were slaughtered in the arena in AD47. Titus had Jewish captives killed in games after the Jewish War (AD66–70) and Constantine I had Frankish captives thrown into the ring in Trier in AD308 to celebrate his victory over them. At the other extreme, one or two debauched emperors, including Nero and Commodus, personally took part in the games. Commodus actually performed in the arena, shooting hundreds of ostriches to demonstrate his *virtus* (courage), but Nero forced senators and equestrians to fight (though not kill) in the arena themselves. Young Roman nobles under the empire sometimes stepped into the arena to fight as amateurs to exhibit their *virtus*, but gladiators on the whole never escaped their low status. Although a few became celebrities, no gladiator ever held high office, although some were used as bodyguards or assassins.

CATASTROPHIC EFFECTS

The Romans imported exotic wild beasts from all over the empire and at times from well beyond their frontiers. In the first millennium BC, great cats such as lions, panthers and tigers still roamed freely in western Asia; in 51BC Cicero's brother, who was governor of Cilicia, was asked to supply panthers from Asia. There were hippopotami and crocodiles on the banks of the Nile and elephants and ostriches could be found north of the Sahara. This rich fauna was devastated over the centuries, as a highly efficient system of capturing and transporting them was established to satisfy audiences in Rome and in other great cities around the empire. By the 4th century AD it was becoming increasingly hard to find animals to satisfy the demands of the arena. Almost none of these great animals, with the exception of a few lions in the Rif Mountains of Morocco, are to be found north of the Sahara or west of India today.

Above: A Roman fresco from the amphitheatre of Mérida in Spain showing a venator *(huntsman) facing a lion with only a spear. Animal games were popular in cities all round the empire.*

Below: Arena substructures, possibly a lion pit, in the amphitheatre of Thysdrus (El Djem), Africa, built c. AD230.

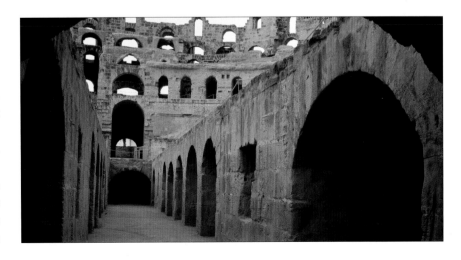

AT THE CIRCUS: CHARIOT RACES

Above: Chariot races in the Circus Maximus, Rome, with the spina *in the centre.*

Below: A quadriga *chariot from a 3rd-century AD mosaic. Only one man rode a chariot.*

Although they had different origins, the *ludi circenses* (circus games) were the *munera*'s greatest rival attraction. Racing with chariots generally took place in the Circus Maximus (the biggest circus). The arena was well-named since it was truly vast, over 660yds (600m) long and 220yds (200m) wide, sited in a natural hollow between the Aventine and Palatine Hills. Progressively adorned, it was given its final form under Trajan, who turned it into a massive structure with three marble-faced arcades built up on vaults. It is estimated it could seat up to 300,000 people, about a third of the city's population.

THE RUNNING OF THE RACES

All drivers belonged to one of four *factiones* (teams) in the imperial period: the Whites, the Reds, the Blues and the Greens. These were sizeable companies or corporations, each with its own stables and team of trainers, coaches, saddlers, vets, blacksmiths and grooms sited in the Ninth Region of the City near the present Palazzo Farnese.

The *factio* normally supported by the people was the Greens, while the Senate supported the Blues. Huge bets were placed on each team or rider. The number of races held per day was 12 under Augustus, but under Caligula – who was almost literally mad about the games – this was doubled and 24 races a day became the standard. Each lasted 7 laps of 620yds (568m), run anti-clockwise around the central *spina* (masonry rib). This was decorated with seven metallic eggs, seven bronze dolphins and other statues. At each end of the *spina* were the *metae* (turning posts).

Most races were for *quadrigae*, four-horse teams. Two-, three-, six-, eight- and even rarely ten-horse teams (*decemiuges*) were known, but the last was normally reserved for egomaniacs like Nero who drove one while collecting every prize at the Olympic Games in AD67. Only the inner pair of horses actually pulled the chariot. The outer pair were only loosely attached by a *junis* (trace), but they were vital to the chariot's stability. Racing chariots were mere boxes, given a little stability only by their driver's weight.

Charioteers wore short sleeveless tunics and leather helmets, and carried knives to cut themselves free from the leads tied round their waists if there was a collision. As up to 12 *quadrigae* chariots could compete in the circus, collisions were common occurrences.

Before a race started, each of the chariots was placed in one of the *carceres* (starting gates). Above them a magistrate presided over the games. When he gave the signal, by dropping a white napkin into the circus, a trumpet sounded, a spring mechanism opened the gates and the chariots were off. Each charioteer strove to attain the best inner position on the left, but fine judgement was crucial. If his chariot wheel so much as touched the *spina*'s stone kerb, it could shatter, wrecking his own and probably others' chariots in the crash. However, if his chariot swung out too far, it risked losing the advantage of the inner position.

As each lap was completed, one of the eggs on the *spina* was lowered to keep count. The last lap was the most excitingly dangerous of all. The winner was greeted with ecstatic applause and given a victor's palm or gold crown and neck chains. To placate the losers among the spectators – and many poorer Romans gambled madly – donations of money would be thrown to the audience and free meals provided afterwards.

As well as the races, there were exhibitions of trick-riding and other less dangerous gymnastic sports. The Circus Maximus also staged wild beast shows.

FAMOUS CHARIOTEERS

Although almost all charioteers were slaves or ex-slaves – and so scarcely higher in Rome's social hierarchy than gladiators – a few became very famous and very rich, both from gifts they received from magistrates and other rich men and also from the fantastic wages they could command from their *factio* for their loyalty.

Supreme among these star charioteers was Gaius Apuleius Diocles, who competed 4,257 times and won 1,462 victories. He wisely retired in AD150 – with a fortune of 35 million sesterces – to a life of quiet philanthropy at Pozzuoli.

Others in the races' heyday – the later 1st and early 2nd centuries AD – also did extremely well. They were known as *milliari* not because they were millionaires – although they often were – but because they had competed more than 1,000 times in the races. Among these *milliari* were Pompeius Musclosus, who competed 3,559 times, and Scorpus, who completed 2,048 races before he was killed.

Chariot-racing, unlike gladiatorial combat, was not banned by the newly Christian rulers of the empire. Indeed, a hippodrome (circus) in the new capital of Constantinople was built right next to the imperial palace in direct emulation of Rome. The bitter rivalry that existed between the Blues and Greens (the other *factiones* were ultimately subsumed) also continued into the 6th century AD and caused the *Nike* (victory) riots in AD529 that almost drove the emperor Justinian from his throne.

Above: Chariot-racing was popular in the provinces too, as this 2nd century AD mosaic from Lyons, then Gaul's greatest city, shows.

Below: A charioteer from the Circus Maximus, Rome, in the 1st century AD. Horses were occasionally raced individually by jockeys as well as being used to pull chariots.

AT THE THEATRE: FARCE, MIME AND PANTOMIME

Above: Two actors wearing masks, from a 1st century AD relief. Roman actors normally wore masks both for comedy and for tragedy.

Below: A 1st-century AD fresco of a tragic actor. This copies a Greek 4th century BC original, revealing Roman links with Greek drama.

Other entertainments the Romans enjoyed were *ludi scaenici* (theatrical performances), performed in the impressive theatres found in almost every city across the empire. These still often splendid buildings give a misleading impression of the importance of theatre, especially of tragedy, to the Romans, however.

In the Roman world, theatre never had the central role that it had in the cities of classical and Hellenistic Greece (500–100BC). This was partly due to the rival attractions of circus and arena which shaped public tastes. Traditional plays without music or dancing were supplemented by musicals accompanied by dancing, spectacular performances, mimes and *pantomimus*. In these lavish displays, spoken dialogue took a distant second place after extravagant special effects.

THE ORIGINS OF ROMAN THEATRE

Roman theatre emerged in the 4th century BC with broad comedy and farce, the *Phlyakes* and the Atellan farces and was performed mainly in southern Italy. The actors wore grotesque masks and padded costumes suiting their stock characters, who had ludicrous names such as Bucco and Maccus (both fools) or Dosennus and Manducus (greedy buffoons). As the play's titles also reveal – *The Pig, The Sow, The Inspector of Morality* – this was unsubtle, rustic humour, with satire directed not at the ruling class – who would have reacted strongly – but at ordinary people.

Rhinthon of Tarento, a Greek city in southern Italy, was one of the most popular playwrights but there was much ad-libbing and many plays were not written down until much later. Farce was the dominant note, forever loved by Italian audiences.

In the 2nd century BC, Plautus and Terence raised the level of comedy. Their plays, concerned with love and its problems, were inspired by the Greek New Comedy, which lacked the satirical bite of Aristophanes and Old Comedy and so was politically acceptable. Only 21 of the 130 comedies attributed to Plautus survive, but his work and that of Terence remained popular with Roman audiences for centuries. However, the Roman comic repertory expanded only slightly later.

Roman poets such as Ennius (239–169BC) also wrote tragedies, but none has survived. However, tragedy was never very popular with Roman audiences. This was partly due to the huge size of many theatres. (The Theatre of Pompey in Rome seated an audience of around 29,000 and the Theatre of Marcellus seated around 14,000.) Such vast structures were not well-suited to plays that required the audience to concentrate carefully on spoken dialogue, no matter how good their acoustics. It was more importantly due to the fact that Roman audiences were generally less well-educated than those of classical Greece and to their wish to be entertained and amused rather than intellectually taxed. Seneca's melodramatic tragedies, so influential in later European theatre, were probably never performed in public at all but reserved for private readings.

BRUTAL THRILLS

Perhaps the fundamental reason why Roman audiences turned away from even the broadest situation comedy lay in their increasing attraction, even addiction to the brutal thrills provided by the amphitheatre and circus.

However, the Romans resourcefully found other uses for their theatres. These involved dance or balletic performances, mime and pantomime. The last was a truly Roman invention, consisting of masked dancers miming a story, which was often based on, or a burlesque of, myth. The first great *pantomimus* (He Who Mimes Everything) was Pylades in Augustus' reign, an actor of great skill who performed most of the action accompanied by music. His performances were so popular that they literally caused riots.

The earlier Roman stage had no actresses and women's roles had been taken by men, as in Greece. Women now appeared on stage, not wearing heavy masks but elaborately made up to add to their appeal. In some later mimes actresses stripped off completely. This was especially useful for enacting mythical scenes such as the rape of Pasiphae, the Cretan queen who became so enamoured of a bull she had a special wooden cow built in which to receive him. (The resulting child was the half-bull, the Minotaur.)

At times, executions in the plot, such as that of *Laureolus*, were literally carried out on criminals. *Laureolus*, who was crucified, remained very popular with Roman audiences for two centuries, as did the *Death of Hercules*, which involved the immolation of a criminal on a pyre.

There is no evidence that these "plays" were staged in the theatre, although they were certainly staged in the Colosseum in AD80. Some theatres in the Eastern half of the empire, where purpose-built amphitheatres were rare, were adapted to stage gladiatorial combats or wild beast displays, even in Athens itself. The citizens of the supposedly more civilized east seem to have got over their initial revulsion, although the first gladiatorial games performed in Antioch reportedly caused a riot.

Actors were considered scarcely better than charioteers or gladiators socially. It was thought demeaning for a Roman citizen to act at all, such things being better left to half-Greek freedmen.

When Nero performed in public theatres, sometimes taking female roles, he deeply shocked all Roman opinion, not just among the nobility. The Christian emperors finally put an end to such entertainments because of their religious associations, which St Augustine found particularly immoral.

Above: Broadest comedy was what most pleased Roman audiences. Buffoonish comic actors such as this one, with his clown-like mask, from a 1st century AD mosaic at Pompeii, were much loved.

Below: Elaborate masks such as this one, depicted on a floor mosaic, covered the faces of all actors except some women in later productions, who even reputedly sometimes stripped.

GAMES AND EXERCISES

Above: Caracalla built (AD 211–17) enormous public baths that included palaestrae (exercise areas).

Below: Roman aspiration to Greek athleticism is exemplified by this statue of c. 100BC, in which a Roman head is stuck on a Greek body.

The Romans regarded keeping fit as a vital part of a citizen's personal regime, but they never fostered a cult of athletics in the way that the Greeks did. Their lack of enthusiasm for nudity was the inverse of the Greeks' near mania for depicting heroic nudity, from soldiers on funerary monuments to stark naked gods, wearing only a helmet. Combined with the ingrained Roman sense of *dignitas*, this meant that no athlete became a civic hero as had happened so often in Greece. However, *mens sana in corpore sano* ("A healthy body and a healthy mind"), as Juvenal put in one of his less satirical satires, was a Roman motto as much as a Greek ideal.

Although ordinary Roman life involved at least a modicum of daily exercise for everyone, rich Romans, unlike their counterparts in classical Greece, seem to have suffered from the diseases of affluence, possibly because they were such very enthusiastic gourmands.

From the later Republic on, Rome was a crowded city notably lacking in public spaces. To counter this, Marcus Agrippa, Augustus' chief minister, built *palaestrae* (exercise grounds or gyms) in the open land of the Campus Martius just west of the old Servian walls where the very first legions had mustered.

Above: Boxing, shown in this 3rd century AD mosaic from Africa, was a popular participatory sport.

Later *palaestrae* were generally attached to the great public baths, so that athletes could bathe after their exercises. At Trajan's Baths, built AD104–9, a corporation or club of athletes was based in the large open-air *palaestra* on the Baths' west side. It flourished for more than 200 years up to the mid-4th century AD. There seems to have been a similar corporation in the Baths of Caracalla, which were built just over a century later.

Wrestling was a popular sport and wrestlers used to smear themselves with *ceroma*, a lotion composed of oil and wax which made the skin more supple. Women also wrestled occasionally, thereby offending the moralistic Juvenal. Dumbbells were popular with men and women as was rolling a metal hoop and running.

BALL GAMES

The Romans had many kinds of ball game. These included the *trigon*, in which three players formed a triangle and tossed the ball back and forth between them; a sort of tennis played with the palm of the hand for a racquet; and the *harpastum*, in which contestants had to catch the sand-filled ball as it flew between players. For all these games except wrestling, a short tunic was worn, for the Romans generally did not like to exercise naked as the Greeks did.

PUBLIC GAMES

None of these simple sports could rival the races or gladiatorial games in popularity, but there were repeated attempts under Nero and Domitian in Rome to enthuse the populace about athletic displays derived from Greek models. This was partly, no doubt, because they were cheaper as well as more edifying to stage than *munera* or *ludi*.

Athletics displays were popular as interval entertainment in the circus, and continued to be important in the Greek part of the Roman empire. Augustus, following the precedents of some earlier philhellenes such as Pompey, founded the Actiaca, games to commemorate his victory at Actium, in which he encouraged young Roman nobles to participate in Greek-style games. He had only fleeting success, however, for the Actiaca is not recorded after AD16 (only two years after the emperor's death).

True to his philhellenism, Nero tried to revive these contests with his Neronia, which were intended to be regular festivals with both athletic and poetic competitions. The senatorial nobility participated in the first but shunned the second, probably because they feared competing directly against the emperor.

It was Domitian (ruled AD81–96), normally considered among the more dourly despotic of emperors, who finally established a cycle of athletic games which endured. In AD86 he set up the *Agon Capitolinus* (Capitoline Games), with prizes for racing on foot, boxing, discus-throwing and javelin-throwing, as well as for eloquence, Latin and Greek poetry and music. He built the Circus Agonalis, now the Piazza Navona, for the sporting

events and an Odeum on Monte Giordano and the Campus Martius for the cultural contests. The poet Martial sang the praises of the winners.

The games survived Domitian's assassination and continued into the 4th century AD. This was partly because they recurred only once every four years, but also because they were aimed at relatively small, select audiences. The Odeum could seat no more than about 5,000 people and the stadium only about 15,000, very small numbers compared to the masses in the Colosseum and Circus Maximus.

Unlike theatres and amphitheatres, these games were not widely copied around the Western empire. In Greece itself the Olympic Games continued to be staged, although the Roman nobility did not compete. Theodosius banned them by AD393.

Above: Two wrestlers in a gymnasium are shown in this relief from the tomb of Caecilia Metella. Wrestling was a hugely popular sport. Wrestlers would smear themselves all over with ceroma, an oil and wax lotion to make it harder for their opponents to grip them.

Left: A sculpture of a Hellenistic athlete, signed by Agasias of Ephesus and dated to c. 100BC. Such fine imported artworks helped shape Roman attitudes to physical beauty.

SCIENCE, TECHNOLOGY AND THE ECONOMY

The Romans, famously pragmatic, were not speculative scientists in the Greek mould, but in the prosperous centuries of the Pax Romana (Roman peace) neither science nor technology stood still. Most scientists were polymaths, interested in many fields. Strabo was a philosopher and historian as well as a famed geographer, while Ptolemy wrote on music and mechanics. Practical matters were not neglected, although they were under-recorded by writers concerned with more prestigious subjects. Water power was exploited more thoroughly, new forms of concrete and glass were developed and ships became far larger. Agriculture, too, made incremental advances and better olive presses were introduced. One revolutionary idea was developed for a tantalizing instant only to be abandoned: Hero's steam engine.

Despite the Romans' complete ignorance of economic theory, there was an immense boom in trade both within and beyond the empire, with new routes reaching as far as India and even China. Massive amounts of wheat and olive oil were shipped across the Mediterranean from Egypt and North Africa. Intercontinental trade on such a massive scale would not recur before the 17th century.

Left: A Roman soldier kills Archimedes, the Greek scientist, during the siege of Syracuse. Fortunately such disasters were exceptional, for Greek science flourished under Roman rule.

STRABO AND GRAECO-ROMAN GEOGRAPHY

Above: Inscribed with many languages, the walls of the Bibliotheca Alexandrina rise in a modern recreation of Alexandria's great library.

Below: The flooding of the Nile was among the mysteries that perennially fascinated Graeco-Roman geographers.

Alexander the Great's conquests as far as northwest India (356–323BC) led to a vast expansion of Greek geographical and scientific knowledge. There followed the golden age of Greek science of the following centuries. This knowledge was collated by Alexander's heirs, especially the Ptolemies of Egypt (322–30BC), who used their vast wealth to turn their museum and library at Alexandria into the greatest scholarly and scientific centre of the ancient world.

A NEW GEOGRAPHY

When Roman power spread – around the Mediterranean, east as far as the Caspian and the Gulf, then north towards the Baltic and Britain – so Roman interest in, and need for, such knowledge grew.

Lucullus and Pompey, the Roman generals who in the last decades of the Republic conquered Eastern kingdoms such as Syria and Pontus, inherited these monarchies' cultural assets and pretensions. Lucullus set up a fine library at Rome with the intellectual spoils of his victories and it was to Rome, the new world ruler,

that Greek philosophers and polymaths such as Posidonius (135–50BC) came, teaching rich Roman students and even a few Greeks. Foremost among the Greek students was Strabo.

Strabo (64BC–*c.* AD21) came from the aristocracy of his native town of Amaseia in northern Asia Minor. Rich and well-connected, he made friends with the Roman nobility, spending long periods in Rome whose government and institutions he admired almost uncritically. "Never before has the world enjoyed such perfect peace and prosperity…cities and peoples united in a single empire, under one government," he enthused. He came to see his work as a two-way bridge between Greek culture and learning and Roman government and authority. Roman power would facilitate the extension of Greek knowledge, while Greek thinking and culture would complement and underpin Roman arms.

Strabo's learning was openly derived from the works of his great predecessors, especially Eratosthenes (275–194BC) – an Athenian who settled in Alexandria to become one of the city's brilliant polymaths – and Posidonius. He wrote in Greek, then the language of almost all scientific thought across the Mediterranean. His first work, a history in 47 books, has vanished completely but he went on to write 17 books on geography which he published in 7BC. These have mostly survived. For Strabo, geography encompassed history, folklore and mythology as well as astronomy and geometry. So, when talking about Palestine and the Jews, he briefly mentions Moses; when discussing Tarento, he notes its legendary and its historical links with its mother city, Sparta.

Strabo accepted the then commonly held view that the Earth was a perfect (immobile) sphere, with all the (known) continents, Europe, Asia and Africa,

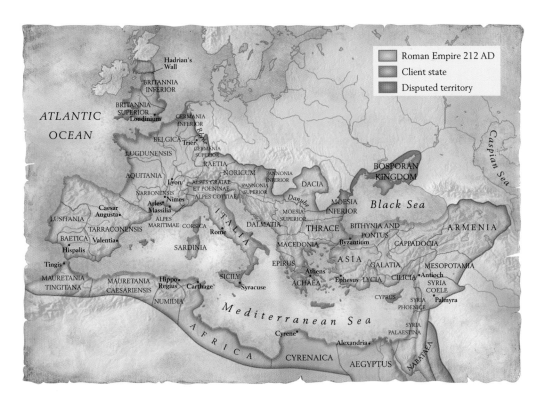

Left: A map of the Roman Empire and its neighbours AD212. As Roman power spread outwards, around the Mediterranean and into northern Europe, Graeco-Roman geographical knowledge grew with it.

forming a single mass surrounded by the encircling waters of Oceanus, a belief as old as Homer. In his first two books he gave reasonably accurate latitudes and longitudes for the cities, oceans and countries he described, ranging from Spain to Assyria (Iraq), from Britain to Ethiopia. He then described each country and people's beliefs and customs.

Strabo seems to have travelled extensively himself, although his description of Armenia suggests that he had a rather credulous acceptance of local beliefs. "Armenia also has huge lakes, one being the Mantiane which, translated, means 'Blue'. It is the largest salt water lake after Lake Mareotis (in Egypt), it is said, extending to Atropatia, and it also has salt works. Another is Arsene, also called Thopitis. It contains soda that cleans and restores clothes, but this ingredient makes the water undrinkable. The Tigris flows through this lake after rising from the mountain country near the Niphates. Because of its swiftness, its current remains unmixed with the lake. Hence its name Tigris, which in Median (Iranian) means arrow."

(*Geography*, Book V.12)

THE ROMAN CONTRIBUTION

Although no later writer under the Roman empire rivalled Strabo in scope and information, he did have successors among writers in Latin, a language still regarded as unsuited for scholarship by many Greek-speakers. For example, Lucius Junius Columella, a Roman of equestrian status from Cadiz who seems to have served as a tribune in the army, wrote a book about geography and agriculture – the two topics were not then distinct – around AD50.

Much the most significant later such writer, however, was Pliny the Elder (AD23–79), an intellectually omnivorous if often undiscriminating writer. In his encyclopaedic works, especially his *Naturalis historia* (*Natural History*) Pliny showed himself the heir of Strabo. He claimed to have recorded 20,000 noteworthy facts about life on earth in its 37 books.

In Books III to VI, Pliny deals with geography and later volumes cover his views on biology and botany. His views, like those of many Latin writers, came to be regarded as almost papally infallible in the Middle Ages.

Below: Roman merchants often ventured beyond the empire's boundaries, but John O'Groats, at Britain's northernmost tip, was Ultima Thule, the furthest land known before the encircling ocean.

ASTRONOMY

Below: The Farnese Atlas, a Roman statue showing the mythical titan who sustained the Earth on his shoulders. Myth and science intermingled in ancient astronomy.

The greatest astronomers of the ancient world were all Greek, although Cicero gave a poetic version in Latin of current cosmogonies in *Scipio's Dream* around 45BC. In the Roman empire Alexandria remained the centre of astronomical science.

Its most brilliant figure was Ptolemy (Claudius Ptolemaus) who wrote in the middle of the 2nd century AD. Ptolemy's work, however, was merely the culmination of a tradition going back six centuries that combined often meticulous observations with daring speculation. Without any form of telescope, all ancient astronomers had to rely solely on what could be discerned of the universe with the naked eye. This inevitably shaped their views. Greek astronomical theories originated with the early Ionian thinkers of the 6th century BC such as Thales, who predicted the solar eclipse of 585BC, and his reputed pupil Anaximander, but during the classical period (480–320BC) astronomy languished. With the establishment of the great library at Alexandria *c.* 300BC, astronomy was revived as a more systematic science.

About 275BC, one especially daring astronomer, Aristarchus of Samos, had suggested that, "The fixed stars and the sun stay motionless and the Earth moves in a circle about the sun", but his ideas were almost universally rejected for what were at the time very cogent reasons. (If the Earth rotated around the sun, centrifugal forces would spin everything off the Earth's surface while the "fixed stars" would have to be unbelievably distant to remain fixed in our view of the sky.)

More typical was Eratosthenes who calculated the Earth's circumference with remarkable accuracy (to within 4 per cent) about 225BC. Hipparchus of Nicaea, probably the finest Hellenistic astronomer, invented varied optical aids a century later, drew up star maps and discovered the precession of the equinoxes, while noting a *nova* (new star).

PTOLEMY'S GRAND COMPILATION
Ptolemy inherited, summarized and consolidated these achievements. He wrote books on mathematics, optics – based on his own experiments in refraction and reflection – and geography. However, his great achievement was his *Grand Compilation*, better known by its Arabic name the *Almagest*, which indicates its amalgamated nature.

Developing Hipparchus' system, Ptolemy provided a detailed mathematical theory to describe the movements of the sun and moon and of the five planets known without a telescope: Mercury, Venus, Mars, Jupiter and Saturn. His system, which was based on his own precise astronomical observations, perfected the geocentric theory of the universe, ingeniously detailing the epicycles and regressive motions needed to make the "wandering planets" fit such a system.

Ptolemy also wrote a book on music, *Harmonics*. This describes several musical instruments but is chiefly concerned with mathematically perfect harmony – an idea

PERSEUS

Algol

TRIANGULUM

TAURUS

CASSIOPEIA

ANDROMEDA

first developed by the mystical philosophers Pythagoras and Plato. He believed that such harmony underpinned the universe and linked it with the human soul. One section is headed, "How the interrelations of the planets are to be compared with those of musical notes.".

Such an apparently workable but mystical view of the cosmos proved hugely influential over the next 1,400 years, both in the Christian and Islamic worlds. Shakespeare was still under its sway in 1598 when he wrote the famous passage in *The Merchant of Venice*, which gives perhaps the most lyrical exposition of the geocentric universe. "Look how the floor of heaven is thick inlaid with patines of bright gold/There's not the smallest orb which thou beholdest/but in this motion like an angel sings/still choiring to the young-eyed cherubins./Such harmony is in immortal souls."

A DANGEROUS SCIENCE
Astrology was one of the Romans' many cultural imports from the Hellenistic East The Romans were very superstitious and heeded soothsayers and other diviners, including *haruspices*, who read the future

in the entrails of sacrificed animals. Accepted almost universally by intelligent people, astrology was a deadly serious business in the Roman empire.

Astrology's basic premises fitted what was then known of the universe and Ptolemy himself related astrology to his own cosmogony. (The five known planets were increasingly identified with their corresponding gods.)

Augustus and his friend Agrippa, young men in 44BC, consulted the astrologer Theogenes at Apollonia in Greece – he predicted amazing futures for both – while Augustus' gloomy successor Tiberius kept his own astrologer Thrasyllus, who established an observatory at Capri. As astrologers were thought to be able to forecast precisely the hour of an emperor's death, it became a crime under the more paranoid Caesars to consult one on such a sensitive subject.

The despotic Domitian had the astrologer Ascletario put to death to confound his prediction that his corpse would be torn to pieces by wild dogs – in vain, for it was – but he entirely believed astrological predictions of the exact hour and manner of his death in AD96.

Above: The Constellation of Perseus and Andromeda, painted by James Thornhill in 1725. The Greeks and Romans viewed the stars' patterns anthropomorphically.

Below: The Ptolemaic system postulated that the Earth lay immobile at the centre of the universe, with the planets and stars circling it in sometimes very complicated epicycles.

WATER MILLS

Above: A fresco from Alexandria showing oxen turning a mill. Such animal-powered mills were very common but not nearly as powerful as water mills.

Below: The remains of a giant water wheel of the Roman era near Cordoba, Spain. Water power was used in Spanish mines for pumping out water and for sluicing rock faces clean of debris.

Among the most enduringly useful innovations that spread around the Mediterranean under the Pax Romana were water mills. They seem to have originated in western Asia and to have been known, if scarcely used, in Greece by the 4th century BC. Traditionally first seen by the Romans in Armenia during their wars against Mithradates of Pontus (89–66BC), they were taken up only slowly at first, probably because of the abundance of slaves in the late Republic and early empire (*c.* 100BC–100AD). However, as the empire ceased to expand so rapidly, supplies of cheap slaves dwindled and water power was exploited to supplement animal and human muscle power for the first time in Western history. It has been calculated that while a slave-operated mill could grind only 15lbs (7kg) of grain per hour and a mule-powered mill about 60lbs (28kg), a typical water mill could grind 330lbs (150kg) per hour. However, as such technological developments were not thought especially interesting or prestigious, they were seldom mentioned by writers or rulers and we have to rely on archaeological evidence which is only now emerging. Who supplied the finance for the larger projects remains unknown, but the state probably played a major role. Windmills do not appear to have been used by the Romans.

THE USES OF WATER POWER

The Romans used water power not only for grinding corn but also for pumping water, especially out of mines, for sawing wood, raising hammers in iron works and washing out mineral deposits. In Spain, whose mines employed thousands of slaves to produce much of the empire's gold and silver, huge reservoirs were built above the workings at Rio Tinto with sluices at one end. When the reservoirs had been filled via aqueducts, the sluices were suddenly opened and a great surge of water washed over the exposed seams to carry away the soil. Sophisticated water-powered pumps were also used to pump out mines, where flooding was a perennial problem.

One of the largest water mill complexes so far discovered was at Barbegal near Arles in southern Gaul. Supplied by a branch of the main Arles aqueduct, 16 mill wheels were set in pairs down a steep slope which dropped about 80ft (23m). This complex probably dates from around AD200 and was involved in supplying the city with its daily bread. It is thought to have ground about 660lbs (300kg) of flour an hour – enough to supply a large proportion of the population of Arles. Only ruins of this industrial-sized complex remain. At the other end of the empire, a Roman-era mill, its huge wheel repaired many times, still turns slowly but proudly at Hama in Syria. However, most mills of the Roman period have long since vanished, leaving no visible remains.

WATER MILLS IN ROME

The first known water mills in ancient Rome were situated on the slopes of the Janiculum Hill. They were powered by the waters falling from the Aqua Traiana, the aqueduct built by the emperor Trajan early in the 2nd century AD. Probably early in the 3rd century AD, a complex of water mills was built in the standard brick-faced concrete across the aqueduct. Parts of the site have recently been excavated, although much remains concealed under nearby streets.

Two mill races branched off the Aqua Traiana and ran parallel to it before rejoining it. There were either three or four mill wheels in the northern mill race and one larger one in the southern mill race.

Mills like these ground Rome's wheat into flour, a necessity as the *annona* (wheat dole) was from the late 2nd century AD normally distributed in the form of baked bread rather than wheat. This particular mill complex seems to have survived the political catastrophes of the 5th century AD. In AD537, Rome was easily captured by the Byzantine general Belisarius and then besieged by the Ostrogoths under Totila, who were trying to regain the city they had ruled for 40 years. When the Goths cut off the city's water supply by breaking down the aqueducts, they also cut off Rome's supply of bread. Ingeniously, Belisarius circumvented the problem by floating water mills placed in boats at a sheltered spot on the Tiber near the island. (The Tiber itself supplied water, along with the city's wells, to the much-reduced population.) The floating mills managed to grind wheat into flour for the populace, according to the Byzantine historian Procopius, who accompanied Belisarius for a time on his military campaigns.

The use of the aqueducts for powering water mills outlasted that of supplying the baths, institutions of which the Christian clergy, by then dominant in the city, disapproved. Water mills for grinding corn lined the Tiber until the late 19th century.

Above: Roman water wheels at Hama in Syria, still turning slowly but effectively after nearly 2,000 years in use. Water mills were built across the empire wherever there was demand and a suitable river.

Below: The emperor Trajan (AD98–117), whose Aqua Traiana aqueduct came to supply water power for Rome's mills.

STEAM ENGINES

Above: Hero of Alexandria, whose many inventions included the world's first steam engine.

Below: Hero, like most scientific polymaths of the Roman empire, had a very practical side, describing in his Metrica ways of measuring land and cubic capacity and in his Stereometrica ways of measuring volumes.

The scientific curiosity and technological experiment of the Roman empire is exemplified by the career of one of the most remarkable inventors of antiquity, Hero of Alexandria, who lived in the 1st century AD. Hero was another gifted Hellenistic polymath – his mention of the solar eclipse of AD62 reveals that his interests included astronomy – but his chief fame is as the author of *Pneumatica*, which lists his varied inventions. Among these are mechanisms which use steam to produce a rotary motion.

This mechanism, which was almost certainly the world's first steam turbine, was more thermodynamically efficient than the piston engines that powered the early industrial revolution and anticipated the steam turbine of Charles Parsons by 1,800 years. Unlike the British engineer's invention, however, Hero's device remained little more than a toy.

HERO'S INVENTIONS

Hero mentioned more than 80 different devices in his main works, *Treatise on Hydraulics*, *Treatise on Pneumatics* and *Treatise on Mechanics* (the last preserved only in an Arabic translation). In these, he described the fundamentals of hydraulics, pneumatics and mechanics as well as many applications, including drinking fountains, self-trimming lanterns, self-filling wine goblets and temple doors that were opened by heat which caused the metal hinges to expand.

The *Treatise on Mechanics* dealt with utilitarian devices such as cranes, hoists (lifts) and presses, while another book, *Metrica*, outlined geometrical methods of measuring land, weights and cubic capacity, including that of the pyramids.

In *Stereometrica* Hero gave highly practical advice on how to measure the contents of *amphorae* (jars) and ships' cargoes. More fancifully, in *Automatapoetica* Hero described two mechanized puppet theatres which he had constructed. In these, miniaturized versions of *The Bacchae*, along with other classical Greek tragedies, were staged. His book on clocks, sundials and other chronometers, *Dioptra*, has sadly been lost.

The inventions which have made Hero lastingly famous were his steam engines. One simply used escaping steam to make a ball jump in the air. The other, more sophisticated version was the *aelopile*. This consisted of a large sealed metal cauldron beneath a hollow metal sphere. Steam from the cauldron's boiling water was forced into the sphere, from which its only way of escape was via two small hooked pipes attached to the top and between which it could rotate freely. As pressure built up inside the sphere, the steam made the sphere rotate swiftly on its axis. This delighted onlookers but most scholars now think it did no more.

Above: Among Hero's many ingenious contraptions was a water dispenser that refilled itself automatically, a useful if hardly world-transforming device.

An intriguing but unsupported legend endures that a vastly scaled-up version of Hero's steam engine was constructed to help lift the fuel up to the top of Alexandria's 400ft (122m) *pharos* (lighthouse). This would have made a real contribution to the city's economy. Whatever the case, Hero the steam-engine maker certainly had no successors and his invention died with him.

INVENTIONS SQUANDERED?
Some writers have seen the Roman empire's failure to develop and exploit Hero's steam invention during the period of its peaceful prosperity as a crushing indictment of Roman – and by extension of Greek – attitudes to manual work in general and to technology in particular. Marxists, among others, have blamed it on the prevalence of slavery, which made the Graeco-Roman elite unwilling to dirty their hands with practical work. In support of this argument, they quote the 2nd-century AD Greek biographer

Plutarch's accounts of Archimedes, the great mathematician and inventor of the 3rd century BC. "Considering the business of mechanics and all utilitarian arts…fit for vulgar craftsmen, he [Archimedes] turned his attention only to things where the beautiful and extraordinary are not mixed with the necessary."

This passage simply reflects the attitudes of Plutarch, a Greek nobleman who shared the prejudices of his caste – views which were still powerful even in the industrializing Europe of the 19th century – but they were not necessarily those of polymath scientists like Archimedes, who invented his famous water-lifting screw, or of Hero, who discussed many practical topics. Real technical and economic factors prevented the development and exploitation of Hero's steam devices.

MATERIAL LIMITATIONS
The ancient Mediterranean world, unlike Britain, Germany and the USA in the 19th century, did not have accessible, abundant supplies of the coal which was to fuel the first two centuries of the industrial age. Even wood was in increasingly short supply by Hero's time, as demand for timber and charcoal led to deforestation. The ancient world's metallurgy, too, was far less advanced than that of Britain around 1800, although Hero had developed the necessary valves and pistons for his steam machines. Most critically, the Greeks and Romans never discovered how to use coal in iron-making. All these factors would have prevented widespread adoption of Hero's devices even if the emperors themselves had supported him. Nonetheless, it remains true that, for the ancient world, entertainment was always the priority, and Hero's spinning automata remained in that category.

Below: Hero not only invented the world's first steam engine but he designed it in the form of a turbine, a sphere with two pipes exiting in opposite directions heated over a fire, far more efficient than pistons. Whether this remained only a toy, or whether it was scaled up to supply the great pharos, *remains unknown.*

MEDICAL PRINCIPLES AND PRACTICE

Above: Funerary stele of Sempronio Hilario, a 1st-century AD Roman doctor.

Below: A woman giving birth using a birthing chair. Soranus of Ephesus wrote Gynaecology, *the one book devoted to women's health.*

Medicine was another field dominated by Greek or Hellenized figures, but it was under Roman auspices, in the imperial capital, that the last great Greek physicians, including Dioscorides and Galen, worked and wrote. The Romans greatly appreciated Greek medical skills. Julius Caesar granted Roman citizenship to any Greek doctors who settled and worked in Rome.

In the 1st century AD, Dioscorides, who came from the Greek city of Anazarbus in Asia Minor, settled in Rome. He had probably served with the Roman army as a doctor and he thrived under the emperors Claudius and Nero (ruled AD41–68). Dioscorides was a brilliant botanist and his book *On Medical Materials* describes plants from many places across the empire, and as far beyond its frontiers as India, that could be used for drugs.

Soranus, who came from Ephesus, spent much of his successful career in Rome in the mid-1st century AD. His *Gynaecology* was the only ancient medical text that was wholly concerned with women's health. He was an eminent surgeon and won the title *princeps medicorum* (First Among Doctors). A typical polymath, Soranus also wrote on philosophy and language.

THE IDEAL PHYSICIAN

Considered the greatest Greek doctor since Hippocrates (*c.* 460–380BC), Galen (*c.* AD129–200) summarized the whole Greek medical tradition. He was born in Asia Minor in Pergamum, where he seems to have started his career tending wounded gladiators. He studied anatomy at Alexandria's famous schools before settling in Rome *c.* AD162 to pursue a dual career as a practising physician and a medical writer. In the first role, he mostly attended the rich and mighty. He became the personal physician of the emperor Marcus Aurelius, the emperor's son Commodus and the wife of the former consul Flavius Boethus. Reputedly, Galen fled the city when it was ravaged by a plague brought back by troops victorious in the East in AD166, but his career and reputation clearly revived on his return.

Galen generally accepted Hippocrates' views that four "humours" control the human condition, both physically and mentally: blood, phlegm, black bile and yellow bile. A person who was ill probably had an imbalance in these humours and treatment was required to return the balance to normal. This might include bleeding, enemas or induced vomiting. Never a revolutionary, Galen incorporated these ideas – which for millennia were almost universally accepted – with more recent Hellenistic research to create his grand synthesis.

In his early days, Galen lectured and dissected in public, normally using pigs' corpses. (Human dissection was not practised by the Romans, although Hellenistic doctors had long been doing dissections in private.) Following contemporary customs, Galen used these anatomical exhibitions to prove preconceived theories, rather than discover new and possibly disconcerting facts. Nonetheless, he was one of antiquity's greatest anatomists. He was also a true physician, taking a holistic view of medicine and of human health.

Galen's works have survived unusually intact – they now make up about ten per cent of all extant classical Greek literature – and deal with many subjects. One is called *The Ideal Physician is Also a Philosopher*, a title which perhaps reflected his own ambitions. Galen aimed above all to establish medicine as an exact yet humane science. He always stressed the importance of exercise, a balanced diet, general hygiene and baths.

Galen acquired such immense authority in his own lifetime and subsequently that all ensuing ages, until at least the 17th century, followed his advice – often blindly. Oribasius, the personal physician of the emperor Julian 200 years later, when told by his master to "Collect all the main writings of the best physicians", started with Galen's summaries on the uncontentious grounds that Galen was the best doctor of them all.

KNOWN BY REPUTATION
There were no medical boards or recognized qualifications for doctors in the Roman empire. Reputation, therefore, was vitally important to a successful doctor. This in turn depended partly on luck, partly on skill and partly on a good bedside manner. Doctors were urged to be dignified but smart in their appearance and to give poor people free treatment. Greek and Roman doctors had almost no effective drugs, although they used a variety of herbal remedies and may have had opium. They therefore laid great emphasis upon listening to their patients.

Asclepieia, shrines dedicated to Asclepius, the god of medicine, received the sick overnight. Patients would sleep in the sacred precincts and there have healing dreams in which Asclepius might

appear and take away their illness. One of the best-preserved of these shrines is at Pergamum. Surgery, in an age without anaesthetics, was only performed when absolutely essential and speed was crucial to avoid death through shock. Medical instruments recovered from Pompeii include probes, catheters, forceps, chisels, scalpels and needles.

Above: A young boy is examined by a doctor in this 1st century BC relief with a Greek inscription.

Below: Building in the Sanctuary of Asclepius, Pergamum, where the sick may have slept, hoping to be cured by the healing god.

PERILS OF URBAN LIFE: PLAGUES, FLOOD AND FIRE

Above: The Tiber, which flows through Rome, was a turbulent, unpredictable river, prone to sudden floods that could sweep across the city.

Below: Plague, graphically personified in this painting by Elie Delaunay of 1869, ravaged Rome repeatedly from AD166 onwards and added to the perils of urban life.

For most people in the world's first cosmopolis, life could be dangerous, unpleasant and short. Public health was probably far better in the empire's smaller towns, but they and the countryside supplied Rome with the stream of immigrants needed to maintain and expand the metropolitan population. Smallpox is the most likely culprit for the plague that ravaged Rome from AD166 for several years and that may have killed 300,000 people (nearly a third of Rome's population). However, epidemics were only the most dramatic of the endemic health problems that dogged the rich and poor inhabitants of ancient Rome.

MALARIA

The worst of these endemic health problems was probably malaria. As Galen dryly commented, doctors practising in Rome had no need to consult the writings of Hippocrates for descriptions of semitertian fever (a stage of malaria among adults), because its symptoms could be observed any day in the city. However, malaria was not recognized as such and the link with the disease-bearing mosquito was unsuspected. Run-off water from the seven hills, overflows from the constantly running public fountains and water-basins and stagnant residue left by the Tiber's frequent floods created ideal breeding grounds for mosquitoes.

Cicero and Livy praised the healthy hills of Rome, where the nobility and later the court lived in spacious houses, in contrast with the low-lying parts of the city, where the large majority of the population lived in often cramped *insulae* (apartment blocks). However, even the rich found it advisable to quit Rome in late summer when malaria was at its most rampant, leaving the poor to their uncertain fates.

No figures are known for Roman malaria deaths, but extrapolation from other parts of Italy similarly afflicted until recently, reveals that mortality rates as high as 60 per cent in the 20–50 age group may have been common.

Malaria would also have increased the mortality rates for pulmonary diseases such as pneumonia, bronchitis and asthma. All are likely to have been as common in Rome as in other cities whose populations approached the million mark before modern medicine.

However, Rome added further unique problems. Although the abundant fresh waters brought in by its aqueducts helped reduce waterborne diseases such as dysentery and typhoid – scourges of metropolitan life until the 20th century – other Roman habits would actually have spread them. People with bowel infections, for example, were urged to bathe their exposed anuses in the public bathwater that other people then bathed in!

Communal as well as private brushes were used instead of paper in public lavatories, another effective way of spreading germs. Further, while the rich few suffered from overeating, many Roman people were chronically malnourished, despite the grain dole. (This was later supplemented by free olive oil, wine and even sometimes pork, but a typical Roman's diet must have left him or her with vitamin deficiencies and this would have further undermined resistance to disease.)

FLOODS AND FIRES

The Tiber provided a useful waterway down to the sea and up into central Italy, but it was a swift, sometimes violent river, prone to dramatic flooding as the snows on the Apennine mountains melted. There were floods nearly every year and major floods in 193BC, when the lower parts of the city were inundated and many buildings collapsed.

As the growing city spread on to the low land in the great bend of the river about the Campus Martius, its inhabitants became yet more vulnerable. In 23BC the Pons Sublicius was swept away – for the second time in 40 years – and for three days the city was better navigated by boat than on foot. Hadrian, among other emperors, tried to improve the embankment walls, but in AD217 floods poured through the Forum Romanum in the heart of the city, sweeping away many startled citizens.

Even worse were the dangers from fire. The *insulae*, blocks of flats up to seven storeys high which housed most of the population, were often jerry-built and prone to collapse (although their construction did improve after the great fire of AD64). Heated by moveable charcoal stoves, lit by smoky oil lamps and built mostly of timber before AD64, they were also extremely flammable. Crassus, one of the late Republic's richest and most powerful men, famously boosted his fortunes by turning up at the site of a fire and buying the still-smouldering site cheap from its stunned owner.

Augustus created a corps of *vigiles*, nightwatchmen/firemen, but they had only limited success. The fire of AD64, which totally destroyed three of Rome's 14 districts, gave rise to Nero's subsequent sensible building regulations. *Insulae* were to have terraces for fire fighting, buildings were to be faced in fired brick and there was to be a minimum distance between them. However even this failed to prevent fire recurring. In AD192 Rome was so devastated by fire that the (half-mad) emperor Commodus proposed to rename the reconstructed city after himself, a project his assassination prevented. The Curia (Senate House) was later destroyed by fire and rebuilt under Diocletian.

Above: The great fire of AD64, here depicted by the 18th-century painter Robert Hubert, was one of the most devastating and also the best documented of the recurrent fires that the inflammable cosmopolis experienced.

TRADE, SHIPS AND NAVIGATION

As Rome grew, it sucked in ever more products from across the globe, establishing new patterns of supply and demand. Although merchant ships had criss-crossed the Mediterranean for millennia, early in the 2nd century AD trade grew to a peak under Roman rule that was not to be reached again for more than a thousand years. This growth is confirmed by the increase in the number of shipwrecks found along major trade routes – such as that past the Aeolian Islands north of Sicily, where many ships bound for Rome sought clearly inadequate shelter from storms – and by the huge numbers of *amphorae* found, the clay jars in which loose liquid substances such as oil, fish paste and wine were transported to Rome.

Below: A woman grocer from Ostia, Rome's great river port, is depicted standing at a trestle table selling fruit and vegetables stored in wicker baskets. The capital city of Rome traded in goods of all sorts.

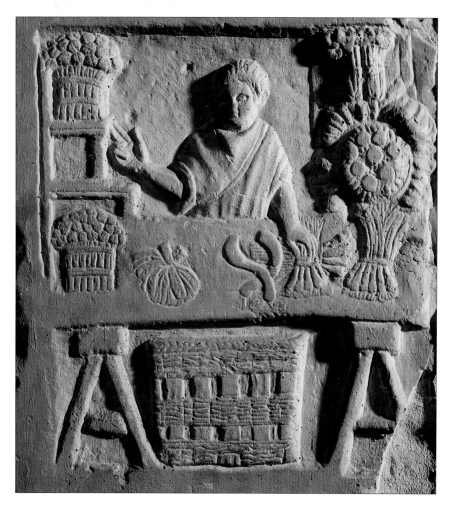

THE MERCHANT CLASS

Members of the senatorial order, Rome's wealthiest class, were banned by the *lex Claudia* of 218BC from owning sizeable ships – those that could carry more than 300 *amphorae* – for commerce was considered debasing. However, some senators probably traded through proxies. Other classes did so openly, the equestrians (knights) particularly benefiting from the boom in trade during the late Republic. So did the numerous *mercatores*, *navigatores* and *negotiatores* (merchants, ship owners and businessmen) who were often not Roman citizens but freedmen.

Emperors, anxious to keep the Roman populace supplied with essential wheat and oil, offered incentives to ship owners. Claudius, for example, promised privileges to anyone owning a ship with a capacity of at least 10,000 *modii* (about 70 tons) who used it to supply Rome with wheat for six years. These ranged from citizenship for non-citizens to exemptions from taxes and burdens such as the *lex Poppaea* which penalized childless couples.

However, most merchants preferred to invest their money in land, which offered security and prestige, rather than found mercantile dynasties. In the 2nd century BC, Cato the Elder voiced the opinions of many Romans for a long time to come when he wrote, "The trader I regard as energetic man, bent on making money; but his is a dangerous career, liable to disaster".

Nonetheless, goods flowed in to Rome, and to other cities and between provinces. Wheat for the million mouths of the metropolis came first from Sicily and Sardinia and then from Egypt and Africa; olive oil came from Spain and Africa; gold and silver from Spain and Dacia; ivory from Egypt and Africa; papyrus and linen from Egypt; textiles and jewels from Syria, and from beyond it silk and spices. Wine, honey and marble came from Greece and

Asia Minor; wool, wheat, wine and pottery from Gaul; tin, wool and lead from Britain; copper from Cyprus and wild animals and timber from Mauretania (Morocco). In the earlier empire Italy produced much wine and pottery and always produced fruit and vegetables. Such a list is far from exhaustive.

SHIPS AND SHIPPING

The *pharoi* (lighthouses) the Romans built around their empire as far north as Dover show the importance they attached to shipping, which was preferred to slow, laborious land transport over longer distances. On the few rivers that were truly navigable, such as the Rhône, regular barge services connected cities like Lyons with the coast, but sea trade was far more important.

As piracy had been almost eliminated under the empire, sea travel might appear to have been relatively safe, but in fact perils abounded, despite the astonishing size of some merchant ships.

The ship that was used by Claudius as the base for the lighthouse of his new harbour near Ostia was vast. About 340ft (104m) long and 64ft (20.3m) wide, with six decks and displacing 7,400 tons, it required a crew of 700–800 men. Pliny the Elder recorded that its main mast was so massive it could only be spanned by four men linking arms and it had a ballast of 800 tons of lentils. This may have been the largest vessel built in antiquity – possibly the largest wooden ship ever, specially made to carry an obelisk from Egypt to Rome – but there may have been other large cargo ships of 3,000 tons ferrying wheat or oil. Galleys, which were highly expensive to crew, were seldom used for cargo.

Although remarkably large, these sailing ships remained technically simple. They generally had only one main mast in the centre with one or two sails and smaller masts at the bow and stern. They never evolved the complex rigging and sails of 17th-century warships or merchantmen. They continued to rely on steering-oars and did not develop rudders like ships of the later Middle Ages.

These lumbering monsters were probably never very seaworthy or manoeuvrable, as they were unable to tack easily with their crude sails. St Paul's famous shipwreck on Malta was not that exceptional. Roman navigators also lacked compasses, sextants and other aids, relying instead on landmarks and the stars in the night sky to determine their position. Fortunately both were often visible in the clear Mediterranean.

Above: A mosaic from Sousse, Tunisia of the 3rd century AD shows a cargo of iron being unloaded from a ship. Heavy goods such as this almost always went by sea, sea transport being generally far cheaper than land transport.

Below: Galley-type ships like this wine-barge from Neumagen on the Moselle, from a 3rd-century AD funerary monument, were used on the larger rivers such as the Rhine, Tiber and Moselle. At sea sailing ships were the norm.

PASSAGES TO INDIA

Above: A cloth merchant presents a client with a length of fabric in a relief from a Christian sarcophagus from Trier of the 4th century AD. Textiles were often traded over long distances.

Below: A harbour scene in a fresco from Pompeii gives a vivid impression of the commercial bustle of a Roman port in the 1st century AD.

Trade grew within the empire but did not stop at the empire's limits. In 116BC a sea captain in the service of the Ptolemy rulers of Egypt discovered the sea-route to India from the Red Sea port of Berenice. Using the monsoon winds that blow across the Indian Ocean, he set sail eastwards in July and returned blown by the reverse winds in December. The routes east were outlined in the *Periplus Maris Erythraei*, a handbook for sailors of the 1st century AD. Greek navigators had by then mostly replaced the Arabs who had once monopolized trade with India.

After Egypt passed into Roman control in 30BC, the lucrative trade grew even faster. From India and other parts of Asia, especially Felix Arabia (the Yemen), came spices, nard, incense, unguents, jewels, cotton textiles and ivory; in return went Roman pottery, glassware, gold and silver. This trade could be fantastically profitable. One consignment alone might be worth three million sesterces and a good-sized ship could carry many consignments. The Greek orator Aelius Aristides (AD117–89) was only slightly exaggerating when he noted that, "Cargoes from India and even from Felix Arabia (the Yemen) can be seen so abundantly as to make one think that in those countries the trees will have been stripped bare and their inhabitants, if they need anything, must come and beg us for a share of their own produce".

Conservative Romans like Seneca muttered about the debilitating effects of such luxury, and Pliny the Elder worried about the adverse economic effect of the outflow of gold and silver to pay for imports – 100 million sesterces a year, he claimed. However, finds of pottery and other artefacts made in the empire along the coasts of western India suggest that Rome's eastbound merchants often exported the empire's products too. The imperial coffers would have profited by the *portorium*, import/export duties levied at 2½ per cent.

THE SILK ROAD

The Indian Ocean was not the only great trade route to the East. Caravans went east across the Syrian desert via the great merchant city of Palmyra – which provided and charged for "protection" and use of its water resources – or down through Mesopotamia, most of which was normally outside Roman control, via the great emporium of Seleucia-on-Tigris, to the Gulf. Spasinochorax at the head of the Gulf seems to have been semi-independent under the Parthian kings, like Palmyra under the Romans. Its great port, which was briefly captured by Trajan in AD116, had regular connections with India and Sri Lanka.

Another route, going entirely by land, struck north across the Iranian plateau to link up with the legendary Silk Road. This is a misleading title, for this was no pan-Asian highway but several different routes taken by camel caravans through central Asia to the western outposts of imperial China. The first Silk Road route was traditionally if unintentionally pioneered by Zhang Qian, an official sent by the Han emperors of China in 135BC to discover and import large horses for the Chinese army. Zhang ultimately succeeded in his mission, although it took him ten years. Traders ventured in his wake, bringing silk west, among other luxury goods, often in stages through the Kushan kingdom in central Asia and via Iran to Syria. Some caravans may have turned south into India, their goods reaching Egypt by sea.

Whatever the route, silk remained an expensive luxury for Romans. Cleopatra VII, last Ptolemy monarch of Egypt and Mark Antony's famous lover, wore silks from China. Such sensual clothing was portrayed as a sign of dangerous decadence by Antony's opponent Octavian, although rich women in Rome soon began wearing silk too. (Sericulture remained a jealously guarded Chinese monopoly until in the 6th century AD, some Byzantine monks under orders from the emperor Justinian managed to smuggle silk worms out of China and inaugurate the Byzantine silk industry.) There were only rare direct contacts between the two distant giants. Chinese envoys arrived in Antioch during the reign of Marcus Aurelius (AD161–80) whom they called Marc-Antun, reputedly mistaking the Syrian metropolis for the imperial capital.

TRADE WITH THE BARBARIANS

Not all trade went east, however. The barbarians to the north traded as well as fought with Rome. Amber had long been imported from the Baltic but Germania – between the Rhine and Vistula rivers – became an increasingly important source of furs, hides, leather, honey and above all, as the empire matured, of slaves.

Scythia (the south Russian and Ukrainian steppe) was another important source of hides, furs and honey. It was also for a long time a major exporter of grain,

helping to feed the cities of Greece. Unfortunately, the migratory chaos of the 3rd and 4th centuries AD disrupted grain-growing in the area just when Constantine's new capital on the Bosphorus would have welcomed it. The problem was dealt with by diverting wheat from Egypt bound for Rome to feed the city of Constantinople.

To the south, the Sahara Desert formed a barrier nearly as effective as the Atlantic for the Romans, who seldom rode camels. Rome had few contacts with sub-Saharan Africa except in Egypt, but there were some routes across the Sahara, and Africa north of the Sahara was still fertile enough to provide wild animals for the circus.

Above: The famous Silk Route from China across central Asia to the Mediterranean ports was eclipsed in economic importance by the sea routes to India via the Red Sea or the Gulf.

Below: A stele showing ship-building in Ravenna, one of the empire's main naval bases.

FARMING

Above: Taking manure to the fields, from a cycle showing the country months in Gaul c. AD200.

Below: Vineyard workers, from a mosaic at Cherchel, Algeria, c. AD100. Wine was produced around the empire.

The great majority of the empire's population (at least 85 per cent at Rome's economic zenith *c*. AD100) always lived and worked on the land. This rural dominance formed the constant background to urban life in the ancient world and farming was always the basis of the Roman economy. Farming, or at least living off the rents and profits from estates, was also considered the most respectable form of existence by the ruling classes.

All senators had to possess land worth at least one million sesterces and most owned far more. Poets such as Virgil and Tibullus praised an idealized rural life that in practice must have been very tough for all but wealthy landowners taking a break from metropolitan cares. However, upper-class Romans were not being entirely hypocritical when they praised country life, for many did take an interest in their estates.

From the 2nd century BC, writers such as Cato the Censor in *De re rustica* (About Rural Matters) gave other landowners advice on how best to profit from their lands in Italy, where *latifundia* (large slave-worked estates) seem to have become common. Cato considered farms as small as 100 jugera (62 acres) as viable but most estates were larger. All such estates strove to be self-sufficient not just in basic foodstuffs but also in carts, tools, harnesses and even in labourers' clothes. The owner should "be inclined to sell and disinclined to buy". Large landowners, however, could afford the outlay of 724 sesterces required for an olive press in Pompeii, for example, while smaller farmers could not.

REPUBLIC OF FARMERS

Traditionally, early Rome was a republic of robust independent farmers, tending perhaps tiny plots but still able to buy their own armour and so rank as Roman legionaries. The influx of slaves and wealth following the Punic and Macedonian Wars of 264–168BC, coupled with the long periods that the Roman soldier-farmer was away from his farm, led large landowners to buy up or simply take over neglected farms, where slaves replaced the doughty Roman peasant.

This view, propagated by the land-reformer Tiberius Gracchus in 133BC among others, painted a dismal picture of an Italy devoured by rapacious great landlords dispossessing little farmers. It is only part of the picture, however. While there certainly were huge new ranches worked by hundreds of slaves, the sort of farm Cato envisaged would have had only about a dozen slaves. Their efforts would have been supplemented by seasonal free labourers working side by side. Another group, the *coloni* (tenant farmers) remained important, as the letters of Pliny the Younger, who made a point of listening to all his tenant farmers' complaints, attest. A few small independent farmers survived alongside their powerful neighbours well into the empire.

Some large estates came to specialize in viticulture, which needed semi-skilled workers; in sheep rearing, which required little labour of any type; and some near Rome in market gardening.

The phenomenal growth of Rome (and other cities) expanded demand, but expanding supply was more difficult. Marginal land in Italy and other well-settled areas could be taken into cultivation but this might make only a marginal difference. Those working such land even in meteorologically good years might consume most of its meagre crop.

In newly conquered Britain parts of the Cambridgeshire fens were drained to grow cereals that were exported to feed the army on the Rhine in the 4th century AD, while in Africa careful planting of olive trees and the collection of every drop of rain allowed agriculture to advance into what had been arid savannah. Southern and central Spain also saw a great expansion of grain and olive cultivation. All these products could also be exported, but Roman wealth created no agricultural revolution. The commonest way to increase farm production was simply to work labourers, whether free or servile, harder.

FARMING TOOLS AND TECHNIQUES
The Romans had good farming tools on a small scale but failed to exploit other technological possibilities. A Roman farmworker would have had excellent axes, spades, sickles, scythes, saws, shears and forks. The multi-purpose vine-dresser's knife, *falx vinotoria*, which was developed from the billhook, has never really been surpassed for its purpose. On a larger scale, the Romans at times used the wheeled plough, which

was Gallic in origin and could turn heavier soils easily, a wheeled threshing-machine with spiked axles called the *plostellum poenicum* and possibly of Carthaginian origin, and two types of reaping machine.

These tools were known and used in Gaul and Britain but they do not seem to have spread round the empire, partly because the Romans remained limited to oxen as draught animals for ploughs and carts. They had failed to develop a form of harness for horses that would allow the animal to draw heavy loads without half-strangling itself. Horses in antiquity therefore only pulled light ceremonial or racing chariots, not carriages, wagons or ploughs.

Farmers normally let some of their arable land lie fallow every other year, to allow it to recover its fertility. This was essential but limited production and illustrates one restriction on Roman power at its most fundamental: it could not easily grow more food.

Above: Oxen being used to plough fields in a mosaic from Cherchel, Algeria, c. AD100. Africa became Rome's chief source of grain and olive oil.

Below: Ploughing with oxen, from a sarcophagus of the 2nd century AD. Oxen were the main draught animals.

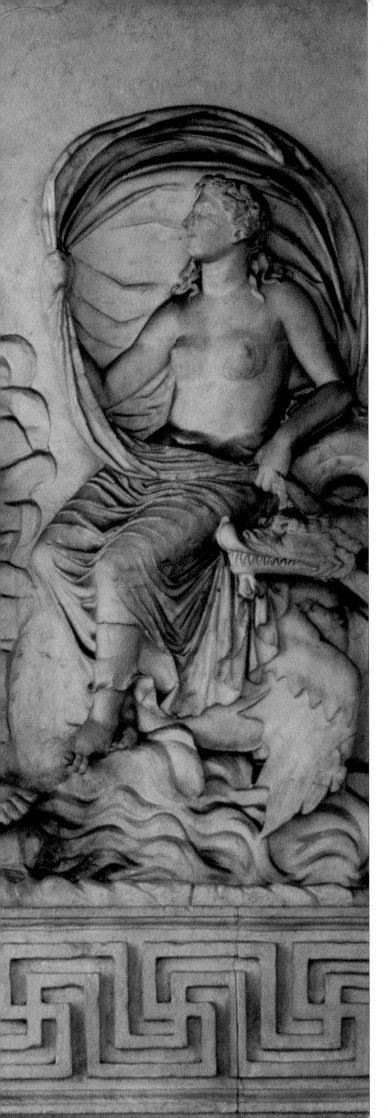

PEOPLE OF ROME

The citizens of Rome of all social classes often showed a preference for *otium*, leisure, over *negotium*, or business of any sort, whether this was governing the empire or running a shop. The cities built or expanded in the centuries of the Roman peace reflected the belief common at the time that the good life was one spent enjoying the amenities of urban life: the baths, theatre, circus, amphitheatre, forum, libraries and the social rounds of dinner parties for those who could afford them.

Most people in the empire in fact lived not in cities of any size but in the country, yet urban life still set the overall tone. Complementing life in the public sphere, the Romans had a strong sense of family and – at least among those who could afford it – of their ancestors.

The position of Roman women, although they were barred from public life, was better in some ways than in comparable cultures, possibly no worse than it was in Britain before the late 19th century. Slavery, a notorious part of the Roman world, was a far more mixed affair than might be assumed. Many slaves were freed and sometimes prospered in business or other work and their sons were later able to hold public office.

Before the triumph of Christianity, the Romans displayed typically level-headed pragmatism about sex, being at times bawdy, at times romantic.

Left: A frieze on the Ara Pacis (Altar of Peace) dedicated in 9BC, showing Tellus (Earth) or Italy, surrounded by symbols of the fertility and harmony restored by Augustus.

MARRIAGE, DIVORCE AND THE POWER OF THE FATHER

Above: A father reclining at ease among his family, a relief from a child's sarcophagus of the 3rd century AD illustrating a Roman paterfamilias' *power at its most benign. The Romans were markedly family-minded, even among the nobility.*

Below: A plan of Rome showing the imperial metropolis at its prime c. AD200. Rome was never a city of grand boulevards or avenues but rather a city of densely packed buildings. filled with political and family intrigue.

Like the Greeks but unlike the early Jews or the Persians, the Romans were always monogamous. The extended family was central to Roman law and society and especially to the real workings of its informal political system.

Although Roman marriage had as its explicit goal the production and rearing of children, among the great political families of the late Republic and empire political motives often dictated unions. Caesar's daughter Julia was married to the much older Pompey to help seal the First Triumvirate in 60BC; Octavia, Octavian's sister, had to marry Mark Antony in an unsuccessful bid to keep the Second Triumvirate together 20 years later, and Tiberius was forced to divorce his adored first wife Vipsania and marry Augustus' only child Julia instead, in a marriage that proved a most disastrous mismatch. Financial motives also played a major role in most noble marriages. However, this did not mean that all were unhappy. Augustus (when still Octavian) married Livia for love rather than politics (she

happily divorced her first husband) and despite his later frequent infidelities, theirs was a happy marriage.

Divorce had become common at least among the nobility by the end of the Republic, although for less exalted people, where personal feelings possibly counted for more, it remained more unusual, although devoid of any stigma. In divorces, children normally remained in their father's custody. However, judging by the feelings expressed on memorials, many ordinary Romans were devoted to their spouses.

THE *PATERFAMILIAS*

The theoretical powers of the father in the early Republic were unbounded. A *paterfamilias* (male head of the household with no living father or grandfather) held *paterpotestas*, powers of life and death over all family members, including his slaves and most of his freedmen. In theory, a father could beat his son although the latter might be middle-aged and hold high office. Family courts dominated by the *paterfamilias* could even hand out death sentences, though these became so rare as to be almost legendary. The *paterfamilias* nonetheless retained the key right to accept – or occasionally reject, if the baby was deformed or of dubious paternity – every newborn child laid at his feet.

Such was the prestige linked to being a *paterfamilias* that senators were hailed as *conscripti patres* (conscripted fathers) and one of the proudest titles held by Caesar and Augustus in turn was *pater patriae* (Father of His Country).

The dependents of a *paterfamilias* could number hundreds for a great household – and later for the *familia Caesaris*, the imperial family, thousands. However, Roman politics in the Republic and the early Principate depended crucially on these extended households for governing

Circus of Caligula
Column of Antoninus Pius
Mausoleum of Augustus
Praetorian Camp
Mausoleum of Hadrian
Temple of Hadrian
Aurelianic Walls
River Tiber
Baths of Diocletian
Baths of Constantine
Stadium of Domitian
Trajan's Forum
Pantheon
Temple of Trajan
Forum Romanum
Basilica of Constantine
Temple of Venus and Roma
Theatre of Pompey
Forum of Augustus
Forum of Caesar
Baths of Trajan
Theatre of Marcellus
Domus Aurea
Colosseum
Domus Tiberiana
Temple of Claudius
House of Augustus and temple of Apollo
Domus Flavia and Domus Augustana
Baths of Caracalla
River Tiber
Circus Maximus

the empire, with slaves or freedmen effectively taking on the role of civil servants. In practice, these vastly extended and powerful dynasties were balanced by more numerous nuclear families, composed just of parents and children. When a *paterfamilias* died – and not many lived long enough to torment their grown-up children for long – his estate had by law to be divided equally among all his surviving children, for primogeniture (in which the first born inherits all) was unknown. Because Roman mortality rates were so high, especially among women giving birth, many people found themselves marrying several times without divorce.

MARRIAGE CUSTOMS

Among the upper classes in Rome, marriages were often arranged for dynastic reasons, but the comedies of Plautus (among others) demonstrate that love was as important for the Romans as for anyone else. Paternal consent was needed, however, for the first informal engagement. This was followed by a banquet at which the man, who was normally about ten years older than the woman, gave his fiancée a large present and the future father-in-law promised a dowry in return.

On the day of the wedding – June was a popular month – the bridegroom arrived early in the morning at the house of the bride with his friends. The matron of honour joined the couple's right hands ceremonially in the *dextrarum iunctio*, an animal was sacrificed and the marriage contract was signed. The groom paid for the reception, which included food, dancing and music. Augustus became alarmed at the increasing extravagance of wedding ceremonies and introduced a sumptuary law to limit the cost of a marriage to 1,000 sesterces. This proved ineffectual.

The bride wore a prescribed hemless tunic-style dress (*tunica recta*) tied at the waist by a woollen girdle (*cingulum herculeum*), with a saffron-coloured cloak over it and an orange veil (*flammeum*). Her hair was dressed in an old-fashioned style, with strands parted using an iron

spearhead. In the wedding procession after the banquet, all the guests escorted the bride to her new home.

The bride herself had three young boys to attend her: one held her left hand, one her right hand and the third carried a torch before her that had been lit at the hearth of her own home. As she approached the bridegroom's house, the torch was thrown away. According to old beliefs, whoever caught the torch was assured a long life.

Upon reaching the bridegroom's house, the bride performed a set of symbolic acts. She smeared the doorposts with oil and then covered them with wool, and ritually touched the hearth fire and water inside the house. She was then helped to prepare for her wedding night by women who had only been married once. Most girls, at least among the nobility, were virgins for their first marriage.

Above: Portrait, possibly of an engaged couple, with a cupid between them, from a fresco in a villa at Stabiae destroyed by Vesuvius in AD79.

Below: Detail of a marriage ceremony from a votive altar of the 3rd century AD, showing a couple formally linking hands.

ROMAN WOMEN

Above: A young woman wearing a wreath of leaves from Herculaneum, c. 10BC.

Women in Rome were barred from playing any role in public life, whether in war or in peace. There were no women consuls, generals, senators or emperors. In this exclusion Rome was in tune with classical Greek precedents but not with the Hellenistic world, where queens such as Cleopatra in Egypt ruled as acknowledged sovereigns. High-ranking women could hope to be powers behind the throne, like Augustus' wife Livia or Nero's mother Agrippina, but they could never assume imperial power in their own right.

In Rome, women were regarded as unfit for that supreme test of Roman *virtus*, military service (which was indisputably arduous). Further, women's voices were thought to lack the carrying power to make themselves easily heard in public places such as the Forum. Oratory was vital to Roman political life even after the end of the Republic.

DOMESTIC POWER

Traditionally women remained always *in manu* (under a man's control), first their father's or guardian's and then their husband's. However, even as early as the 3rd century BC such constrictions were being evaded by marriage contracts that specified the dowry the woman could take back with her if the marriage ended in divorce or death. Divorce could be initiated by either party without formality, although aristocratic marriages with political implications remained more complicated.

Left: Cornelia, mother of the Gracchi brothers, who held the first known literary salon in Rome.

A Roman *matron* (married woman) ran the household, controlling the domestic slaves and holding the keys of the house. By the age of 25 she could normally manage any property that she had inherited independently, which made her better placed than women in early Victorian Britain. When her husband was away, a wife took control of family affairs. Domestic duties, such as looking after the children and the household, traditionally included making clothes for the family even for wealthy women. *Lanam fecit* (she made wool) was a common tribute to a deceased wife. However, by the later Republic women were joining men at dinner, that central event in convivial Roman life, where they acted as hostesses. This was in marked contrast to their seclusion in Greece, as Cornelius Nepos, the first extant Latin biographer, noted. Although girls received less in the way of formal education than their brothers, by the 2nd century BC many upper-class Roman women were literate, as is shown by the life of Cornelia Gracchus.

INCREASING FREEDOM

Cornelia, daughter of the great Scipio Africanus who had defeated Hannibal, was among the first newly independent women (although scarcely liberated in the modern sense). She married Tiberius Cornelius Gracchus and among her progeny were the famous if ill-starred reformers Tiberius and Gaius Gracchus.

Cornelia took control of her six sons' education – a task traditionally reserved for the *paterfamilias* – and selected the finest Greek tutors for them. She was the first woman known to have held a literary salon in Rome where poets, philosophers and politicians gathered. As a widow she was so widely admired that Ptolemy VII, the Hellenistic king of Egypt, asked (unsuccessfully) for her hand

Left: A mother breast-feeding her child in a vivid fresco from Pompeii. The maternal role was inevitably considered women's chief occupation, although aristocratic women in fact had relatively few children by the late Republic.

in marriage. Although she was later content to be known as "the mother of the Gracchi", Cornelia deserves fame in her own right as a pioneer of women's independence. By the 1st century BC, other women were enjoying considerable freedom. The married aristocratic woman, who Catullus addressed as Lesbia and passionately loved, clearly had enough independence to have affairs.

Augustus tried to restrict women's freedom in his restoration of public morality. This re-emphasized gender differences, in deliberate contrast to the perceived immorality of the late Republic and to Cleopatra's "Eastern" court which had allegedly corrupted Anthony. Augustus even banished his daughter Julia and her daughter (also called Julia) for sexual immorality. Here he applied his own laws, for under the *Lex Julia* of 18BC, adultery had become a serious crime, at least for women, who could be banished, lose half their dowry and be prohibited from remarrying. Women now went to the public baths at different times to the men and were restricted to high seats in the theatre and amphitheatre. (They continued to sit with men in the Circus, however, and Ovid recommended the Circus as a good place for young men and women to meet and flirt.)

WORKING WOMEN

Most women could never be empresses or wives of great politicians, but some still made their way in a male-dominated world. A few managed to be accepted as doctors – there is a funerary inscription in Latin for a female doctor, Asyllia Polla, from Roman Carthage – although later women seem to have been excluded from practising medicine for a time. As no formal medical body existed to regulate doctors, this may have reflected changes in the social climate.

Some women worked as bakers, pharmacists – another then unregulated profession – and shopkeepers, either with or without their husbands. There was only one woman Latin poet of note, Sulpicia, niece of an important politician *c.* 20BC, and almost no opportunities for women to make their voices heard in public life.

Below: A relief showing a woman pharmacist in her shop. Pharmacy, like medicine, was a totally unregulated profession and so one which women could enter and where they could, with luck and industry, prosper.

CHILDREN: EDUCATION AND UPBRINGING

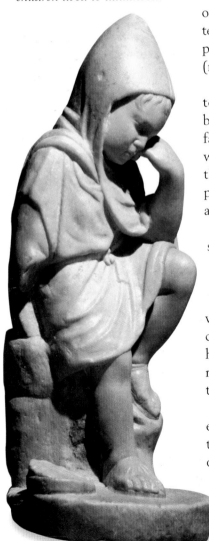

Above: Children play with walnuts in a relief from Ostia of the 2nd century AD, then a thriving harbour city.

Below: Sculpture of a sleeping child. Very high rates of infant mortality meant that few children lived to adulthood.

In the 2nd century BC, Cato the Censor boasted, perhaps untruthfully, that he had taught his sons everything from reading to swimming but, over time, education in richer households passed from the hands of fathers to professionals, slaves and free, as Rome filled with well-educated Greeks. However, Roman education remained generally unsystematic and for girls was almost non-existent beyond a basic level which was normally taught at home.

AN AD HOC EDUCATION SYSTEM

Primary schools, which were mostly private and which only some Romans attended, taught the three basic subjects of reading, writing and arithmetic. Most teaching took place in porticoes or similar public areas such as the great *exedrae* (recesses) of Trajan's Forum.

Teaching was mostly a matter of learning texts by rote, with underpaid teachers beating lessons into boys. Among wealthier families, a *paedagogus*, a slave-tutor who was usually Greek-speaking, took care of the education of boys. Supposedly his pupil's master, he was in reality his slave and accompanied him everywhere.

Relatively few pupils progressed to secondary education where a *grammaticus*, again often a Greek-speaker, taught Latin and especially Greek literature. The poet Virgil was grateful that his parents, who were only moderately prosperous provincial farmers from the Po Valley, had given him a good education in Milan and Rome rather than at the local school full of "centurion's sons with their satchels".

Although emperors such as Trajan established chairs for lecturers paid by the public purse in Rome, there were only sporadic attempts to establish an educational system across the empire. Hadrian, for example, tried to encourage primary schooling in remote parts of the empire by offering tax concessions to school masters willing to teach in the villages of the mining region of Vipasca in Lusitania. Even fewer students went on to higher education, where a *rhetor* taught the vital art of public speaking. The Senate at first actually discouraged the spread of higher education in case it undermined its own monopoly on power.

After being taught by a *grammaticus*, some young Roman nobles went to one of the acknowledged Greek centres of cultural excellence to learn not only rhetoric but philosophy. Athens was long acknowledged as the greatest of these but it always lacked a proper university in the modern or even medieval sense, for private lecturers competed openly for students.

Marseilles' enduring Greek character in the 1st century AD made it a centre of learning. The mother of Agricola, who became a great general, sent him there to complete his education. Later, a few Western cities such as Bordeaux acquired universities, but their prestige never rivalled that of medieval Bologna or Oxford or contemporary Harvard.

THE LANGUAGE OF LEARNING

Latin was the language of most of Italy and later of the Western provinces, but not of every inhabitant of polyglot Rome, let alone of the empire. Greek was also very widely spoken. Almost all cities in the Eastern half of the empire, and most in Sicily and southern Italy, were at least partly Greek-speaking, while until *c*. 50BC Latin literature hardly compared with Greek.

For a long time, the majority of Romans acknowledged, with varying degrees of reluctance, the supremacy of classical Greece in the cultural field, while considering contemporary Greeks their political and social inferiors. So important was a fluent knowledge of Greek to an educated Roman thought to be that the Roman rhetorician Quintillian (*c.* AD35–100) suggested that upper class boys should learn Greek *before* they learnt Latin. Quintillian, who wrote on education, was given a salary by the emperor Vespasian. As tutor to Domitian's nephews, he soon became the acknowledged head of the teaching profession in Rome, so his views were hardly those of an outsider.

Latin remained, however, the language of the army, the administration and the law. In the 4th century AD, a school teaching law in Latin was actually established in Beirut in a long-Hellenized part of Syria. Although many Greeks must have known a little Latin in order to deal with officials and soldiers, they hardly mentioned it. One exception was Ammianus (*c.* AD330–94), a native of Antioch who learnt Latin to write stirring histories of the Persian wars in the mid-4th century in a style that was modelled on Tacitus and Livy. Apuleius, the Latin-speaking author of *The Golden Ass*, makes his central character a Greek-speaker who (comically) apologizes for his poor Latin.

COMING OF AGE

Between the ages of 14 and 19, usually at the age of 17, the Roman male came of age, putting on a new white *toga virilis* to mark his status as a full citizen. He then went to the *Tabularium* (Records Office) with his family to be officially enrolled, after which a family banquet was held in his honour. High infant mortality meant that many children died long before this age, however. In the Republic, young male citizens were liable for military service.

Above: A 4th-century AD class from Gaul, showing a teacher, flanked by pupils, all in fine, probably wickerwork armchairs, while a late arrival tries to apologize. The students are reading from papyrus scrolls.

Below: A woman baths a child in a mosaic of the 3rd century AD from the House of Theseus in Paphos, Cyprus.

SLAVES AND FREEDMEN

Above: A slave serves wine in a bas-relief of the 2nd century AD in Rome.

Below: A mural from Pompeii showing two young women and a younger girl attended by a slave hairdresser. Rich Roman women usually had many domestic slaves to look after their every need.

The traditional view of the wealth and power of the Roman empire existing only through the sweated efforts of wretched slaves can be very misleading. The truth is more complicated, for the relative status of "slave" and "free" might appear strange to modern eyes.

THE STATUS OF SLAVES
A Roman nobleman might have a Greek-speaking slave as his secretary or clerk, another as a librarian or tutor to his children and another as bailiff or overseer of his land. These were often positions of importance and responsibility and some-times of real if limited power. As Romans prided themselves on *manumission* – formally freeing worthy slaves – and as other slaves could at times save enough money from doing work on their own to buy their freedom, the number of freedmen, especially in Rome itself, was large. A few,

like the gross Trimalchio – a fictional but half-plausible character from Petronius' novel *Satyricon* (*c*. AD64) – became multi-millionaires. Others, like Narcissus and Pallas, the emperor Claudius's principal secretaries, indeed rose to become some of the most powerful men in the empire, although their influence over the malleable emperor was resented by the Roman aristocracy. Freedmen's sons could hope to rise to be magistrates, while freedmen themselves often became priests in a local cult in the provinces.

Slavery in ancient Rome was therefore radically different from its last manifestations in the Western world, when millions of enslaved Africans remained slaves just because of their colour. Most slaves who flooded into Rome as it conquered the Mediterranean world in the years after 260BC would have looked broadly similar to the Romans themselves, with darkish hair and olive skin. Those from the Eastern cities were often at least as educated and cultured as their Roman masters, sometimes more so. As the empire developed, less sophisticated Germanic tribes from across the Rhine and the Danube became the chief source of slaves and there was no more such cultural enrichment. The Romans always snobbishly disdained everything about the Germans except their fighting qualities (despite Tacitus' seeming praise for the Germans' love of primitive freedom). There are few depictions of black Africans in Roman art, which suggests that the Romans had only a few slaves from sub-Saharan Africa.

Precise figures are lacking, but probably nearly a third of the population of Italy in the 1st century AD were slaves, while at that time about half Rome's own population may have consisted of slaves and freedmen. A proposal in the Senate in the 1st century AD that all slaves should

*Left: Making a will: a
funerary stele for man and
wife from the 1st century* AD,
*showing a slave with a
counting tablet on the left.
Slaves were sometimes given
their freedom by their masters
in such wills. This was a strong
inducement to good behaviour.*

wear a uniform to identify them was rejected when it was realized that this would reveal how numerous they were. Across the whole empire, however, the proportion of slaves to non-slaves was close to 10 per cent. Slavery probably peaked at the end of the Republic and the beginning of the empire and then very slowly began to decline, as the wars of easy conquest petered out. Such wars were the chief source of slaves, although piracy, kidnappings and abduction of foundlings, along with *verna*, the children of slaves born in the household, provided other major sources, as did trade with peoples beyond the empire.

THE GROWTH OF SLAVERY

Slavery had always existed in Rome as in almost every ancient society. The Twelve Tables of the Law of 451–450BC stipulated that Romans were only to be sold into slavery "across the Tiber" (outside Rome). A common form of early slavery was the *nexus*, in which a Roman citizen who had become indebted lost his freedom to his creditors. Debt bondage was abolished by the *Lex Poetelia* of 326BC.

Soon after, Rome began the series of wars of conquests that provided it for a time with seemingly inexhaustible supplies of unfree labour. About 11,000 Samnite war captives were reportedly enslaved

after their final defeat in 290BC. But the fleets the Romans raised to fight the First Punic War in 260BC were rowed mostly by free men – usually citizens of the lower property classes – as were most later fleets of galleys. A perennial disadvantage of owning slaves was that they needed feeding all year round even when not working. War galleys, for example, spent more than half the year ashore.

In 167BC, the systematic destruction of the kingdom of the cities of Epirus (northwest Greece) reputedly brought 150,000 slaves as war captives to Rome, probably helping to raise the intellectual tone of the whole city. Less accomplished, and so cheaper, were the 65,000 Sardinian slaves put up for sale in 177BC. The slave markets must at times have faced gluts. Cato the Censor noted with disgust about this time that pretty slave boys were fetching higher prices in the slave market than sturdy ploughmen, reflecting supply and demand. In the 1st century BC, Strabo estimated that the great port at Delos in the Cyclades was capable of handling 10,000 slaves a day (although this was a maximum, not a norm). Strabo also noted that slaves were one of Britain's main exports. Gallic chieftains reputedly sold a slave for a single amphora of Italian wine. Slaves were among the main booty of Caesar's Gallic wars (58–51BC) soon afterwards.

*Below: A slave bringing in
food for a banquet, from a
mosaic from Roman Carthage
of the 3rd century* AD. *The
more attractive or intelligent
slave could hope for such
domestic service. Those lacking
such charms often ended up in
the mines or on farms.*

ASPECTS OF SLAVERY

Above: The mines of Las Medulas in Spain where many slaves were worked to premature deaths.

By the end of the Republic, owning a slave or two was as common even for quite ordinary Romans as owning a car is today, and scarcely more reprehensible. Often such slaves would do domestic duties or work on the farm or in the family business alongside free hired labourers, and they could be hard to tell apart from poor citizens. In contrast, great nobles could have hundreds of slaves around them in their houses and possibly thousands more working their *latifundiae* (great estates).

THE WORK OF SLAVES

Slaves performed many different tasks in the Roman world and so did not form a single economic or social class. Their jobs and their social status differed greatly, ranging from the highly educated Greeks whose intellectual powers were appreciated by Roman nobles who exploited them as secretaries, librarians, tutors or clerks – Epictetus the philosopher being the outstanding example – via attractive young girls and boys who were sexually exploited, to those at the very bottom of the servile scale. These last, lacking beauty, intelligence or any other notable qualities, could find themselves condemned to crushing work on the land or in the mines.

Left: A slave being freed, showing his progress from prostrate subjection to shaking his ex-master's hand.

Many farm and mining slaves were appallingly treated. Pliny the Younger talks of chain-gangs of agricultural slaves who had "speaking" iron collars forged around their necks. These collars, as uncomfortable as they were demeaning, requested the finder to return the slave to its rightful owner like a dog. Even worse were conditions in the mines where slaves worked alongside criminals. Although tiny quantities of coal were mined in Roman Britain, these were for the most part metal mines. Some of the largest and most profitable mines were imperial property. The copper mines in Cyprus and gold, silver and lead mines in Spain were huge. The biggest industrial undertakings in the whole empire, they employed many thousands of slaves who were worked to early deaths underground.

Elsewhere, in the fertile province of Africa for example, even large estates seem to have been worked mostly by free tenant farmers. In much of the empire free seasonal labour supplemented slaves at busy times like the harvest. Slavery therefore, while part of Roman culture, was not always fundamental to agriculture but it was to quarries and mines.

REVOLT AND REBELLION

Unsurprisingly, slaves sometimes revolted. In Sicily, where huge *latifundiae* worked by slaves were established early on, slave revolts in 135–132BC and again in 104–100BC threatened Roman control of the island.

In the second revolt, a Greek-speaking slave calling himself Antiochus briefly established control over almost all Sicily. Spartacus' gladiators' revolt of 73–71BC attracted many other slaves far closer to Rome. In the troubled 3rd century AD, much of central Gaul was for years in the hands of the *Bagaudae* (literally, brigands), who even set up their own courts.

Household slaves very seldom turned on their masters. The case of the senator Larcius Macedo, who was attacked by his domestic slaves *c.* 100AD, was shocking to his contemporaries precisely because it was so exceptional.

MANUMISSION

Something which impressed Greek visitors to Rome was the ceremony of *manumission*, in which Roman slave owners gave particularly favoured slaves their freedom. This often formed part of the owner's will.

With freedom normally came admission for the newly liberated to Roman citizenship. However, as *manumission* was granted through *paterpotestas*, the power of the head of the family, freedmen were normally considered bound to their former owners by ties of gratitude, taking their names and joining their patron's *clientalia*, network of retainers. Obviously, *manumission* was less significant for a small builder or blacksmith who only manumitted one or two exhausted slaves in his will, than for a noble who grandly freed many slaves. The promise of manumission must have helped to encourage good behaviour among slaves.

Although there were no famous abolitionists of slavery in the ancient world, the Greek philosopher Aristotle (384–322BC) did not consider slaves inherently inferior to free citizens and both the Stoics and Epicureans considered slaves capable of philosophy. For Christians, even the most degraded of slaves had immortal souls, an important part of their religion's early appeal, but richer Christians owned slaves like everyone else.

Every slave owner retained power of life and death over his human property, although more humane emperors tried to mitigate abuses of this power. Augustus saved the life of a slave boy whose irascible master, Vedius Pollio, had wanted to feed him to the lampreys for breaking a precious glass; and Claudius banned the

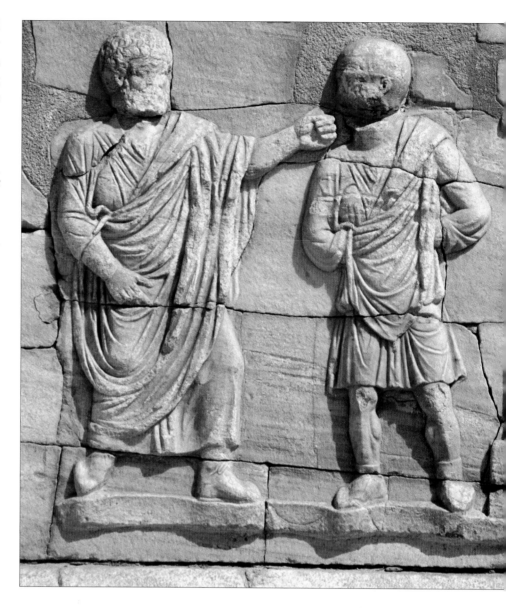

practice of masters reclaiming sick slaves left to die on the island in the Tiber, saying that if slaves recovered their health they also recovered their liberty. Domitian forbade the castration of slave boys for sexual purposes (although slaves still had no defence against their owners' sexual demands) and Hadrian stopped slave owners handing their slaves over to the gladiatorial schools as a punishment and made executing slaves dependent on the approval of the prefect of the *Vigiles* (night watchmen).

Slavery, if waning in importance, as an institution, survived both the gradual conversion of the empire to Christianity in the 4th century AD and the end of the West Roman empire in the 5th century AD.

Above: Relief from the theatre of Sabratha, showing a scene of a slave rebuked by his master, c. AD180.

Above: Claudius, an emperor who tried to limit the mistreatment of slaves.

BUSINESS AND COMMERCE

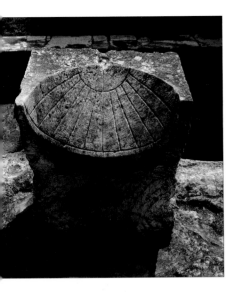

Above: A Roman sundial from Utica in Africa. The Romans, who lacked mechanical clocks, relied on sundials, hourglasses and waterclocks to tell the time.

Below: A Roman relief depicting a vendor of pillows, furniture coverings and textiles. Many poorer Romans found underpaid work in such small-scale service industries.

Like most aristocracies, the Roman nobility liked to advertise the fact that they could enjoy a life of leisure as well as their riches. In the later empire, senators were excluded from politics and the army although many still had their large estates to run. *Otium cum dignitate* (cultured, dignified leisure) was always their motto.

HARD WORK

Earlier, the senatorial order had been closely involved in public affairs during both the Republic and Principate. This is well illustrated by the careers of two men who lived near the empire's apogee: Pliny the Younger, who died *c.* AD112, probably in office as proconsul of Bithynia, after a career as a soldier, lawyer and a consul; and Sextus Julius Frontinus, who died at the age of 70 in AD100 while still the highly effective *curator aquarum* (controller of Rome's water supply) after a career as a consul, soldier and imperial administrator. Conscientious emperors – and most emperors were conscientious if not brilliant rulers – were often also grossly overworked.

At the other end of the social scale, the poorest among the free laboured until exhausted for a pittance. The supposedly pampered populace of Rome, although given *panem et circuses* (free bread and circuses), had to find other means to pay Rome's notoriously high rents. Many did odd labouring jobs, among which portering the huge quantities of food the capital demanded must have been one of the most important, along with working on construction. However, most Romans tried to divide their day clearly into *negotium* (literally: "not leisure", or business) and *otium* (leisure) – the latter having the real appeal.

Although winters in Rome can be chilly and wet, life for men was lived in the open as much as possible or at least in the shelter of porticoes, principally those surrounding the Forum Romanum, and the adjacent imperial fora. The Forum Romanum, at the heart of Roman public life, was also initially the site of the food markets, but these were moved out closer to the Tiber to the Forum Boarium (Cattle Market) and Forum Holitorium (Vegetable Market). This segregation of the messier aspects of commercial life from the ceremonial and social happened in other cities, such as Pompeii and Pozzuoli, and Lepcis Magna and Timgad in Africa, for Romans wanted to make each Forum a splendidly adorned centre of civic pride. In the Forum Romanum male citizens, supposedly all dressed in togas, would meet to discuss matters and renew their ties of mutual obligation. Women remained at home.

THE WORKING DAY

Business of many kinds, of which commercial business in the modern sense was only a part, occupied the first part of the day. This began early, often at first light. Although the Romans had numerous public holidays, they did not have a specific day of the week as a day of rest as Sunday is today for many of us. However, the hours of their day, delimited chiefly by sundials, varied according to the time of year, both the hours and the day being far longer in summer. The Romans relied on sundials and water clocks copied from the Hellenistic world. Men working in particular trades, most of which had their own guilds, went out to work. The building trade was one of the most important in Rome up to the 3rd century AD, but there were also guilds of butchers, fishmongers and bakers, all of which held regular dinners.

In the morning every patron, who might be a powerful noble but who might also be considerably lower down the social and political ladder, would meet some of his *clientalia*, his retainers or supporters. Almost every citizen in Rome was tied by bonds of *obsequium*, mutual obligation, from the poorest man without work to great nobles. Only the emperor had no one above him. Clients were expected to vote for their patrons in return for the occasional gift, which often included daily *sportula* (small gifts of free food), as well as more substantial occasional gifts such

as a new toga for appearing in public, support in legal or social problems and financial aid at times. Later, after elections of magistrates were abolished in AD14, clients were still expected to accompany their patron on his rounds through the city, perform little tasks for him and add to his general glory. Juvenal attacked the way each morning Rome's streets filled with clients hurrying to pay their respects in the *domus* (house) of their patron.

Above: The Forum Romanum in the 4th century AD, seen from the area of the House of the Vestal Virgins.

Below: A bas relief of the 2nd century AD showing a butcher hacking meat in his shop in Ostia. Many Romans were small shop-keepers.

LEISURE AND HOLIDAYS

By midday, most Romans would have been up for six hours or more and would have hoped to have accomplished their *negotium* (business) – on days when business could be conducted at all. There were numerous *dies nefasti*, days of ill omen when judgements could not be made and when public assemblies could not be held.

DAYS OF ILL OMEN

On the many such inauspicious days the Romans celebrated religious rites such as the *Ludi Apollinares* dating from 208BC which ran from 6–13 July, or the *Ludi Victoriae Caesaris* which commemorated Caesar's military conquest of Gaul from 20–30 July.

The purpose of these displays was not to encourage mass idleness and drain the public coffers but to celebrate the power of the Roman people and honour the appropriate gods. The latter included deified former emperors. By the reign of Claudius (AD41–54) 159 days a year were *dies nefasti*. He and subsequent wise emperors such as Vespasian tried to reduce the number. Marcus Aurelius restored the business year to 230 days.

LEISURED AFTERNOONS

Even on *dies fasti* (when judgements could be made), the Forum emptied of citizens conducting business as the afternoon wore on. Most drifted off in search of entertainment in the warmest part of the day. One important event for the poorer citizens – who formed the majority of Rome's inhabitants – was the monthly distribution of the *annona*, the grain ration, which was handed out at the Porticus Minucia. By AD200 this came in the form of baked bread and was later supplemented by wine, oil and pork.

Far more spectacular were the gladiatorial games, the races at the circus and performances at the theatre which diverted the Roman people. As these huge public structures could contain much of the city's population – the Circus Maximus could seat about 300,000 people, the Colosseum and the Theatre of Pompey about 50,000 people each – this was truly mass entertainment.

The other enormous draw was the public baths. There were 170 in Rome by 33BC and 856 by AD400, but by the 4th century AD the small establishments had long been eclipsed by the 11 huge imperial baths, the *thermae*, that were some of the grandest Roman buildings. Starting relatively modestly with the Baths of Agrippa of 25BC, these assumed majestic form with the Baths of Trajan, which opened in AD109. The even larger *thermae* that followed in the next two centuries – the Baths of Caracalla, Diocletian and Constantine – expanded the same concept, which was copied in the provinces.

Lavishly designed and decorated, these complexes combined the functions of gyms, health centres, swimming pools, libraries, restaurants, meeting places and bordellos. Romans in cities around the empire would spend leisurely afternoon

Above: Gambling in bars and other public places was a common Roman pastime. These dice players are from a north African mosaic of the 3rd century AD.

Below: A wealthy Roman woman going to the baths accompanied by her servants, from a mosaic at Piazza Armerina, Sicily, of the 4th century AD. Women usually had different bathing times to those of men.

hours exercising in the *palaestra*, bathing in the *caldarium*, *tepidarium* and *frigidarium* (respectively the hot, warm and cold baths), swimming in the open-air *natatio* (swimming pool), walking in the gardens, relaxing, and enjoying relationships of varying degrees of intimacy with other bathers. Some women joined men at the baths. But as there were designated hours for women, it was probably only women of ill-repute who bathed with the men. When early Christians fulminated against the amount of time wasted sinfully at the baths, they were attacking less physical cleanliness – although Christian ascetics frowned upon washing, preferring to mortify their dirty flesh – than this openly sybaritic aspect of Roman life.

SHOPS AND BARS

Almost all of Rome's *tabernae* (shops) were small and specialized. They consisted of one room, often at the ground level of an *insula* (apartment block), with a wooden or masonry counter across the entrance that was closed off at night by shutters. They normally had a mezzanine floor above. Most *tabernae* lined the narrow streets. Bakers would have grain storage space, mills and baking ovens at the back of the shop. One shop in Ostia has murals of its goods behind the counter, such as grapes and olives. Another depicted on a terracotta plaque shows a poultry shop with baskets of eggs on the counter. A few jewellers and shops selling luxury goods remained in the Forum Romanum. Domitian tried to clear the streets of the clutter of shops, with limited success. However, complexes of shops were developed early at Terracina, and Livy mentions an early specialized food market near the Forum Romanum. Much the most splendid complex of markets and offices was Trajan's Market, rising above Trajan's Forum. This is thought to have offered covered shopping inside one of Rome's most remarkable buildings.

Rome and other cities also had plenty of bars where men could drop in for a quick drink or a snack. Some were tiny,

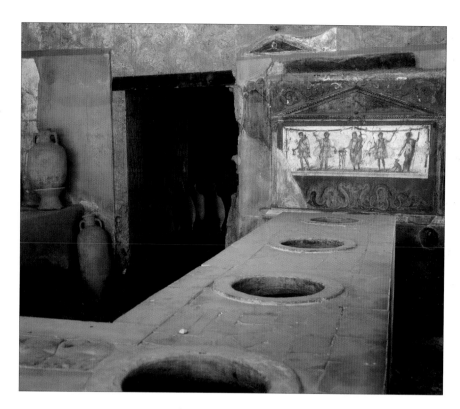

little more than holes in the wall, but others, such as that found in the House of Amphitrite in Herculaneum, had seating with *amphorae* stacked in wooden wall racks. Romans liked to gamble as well as drink in such bars, while snacking on olives, bread, seafood and sausages. There were also modest restaurants, such as that found in the Via di Diana in Ostia. This had shelves and counters lined with second-hand marble and simple tables.

Above: A tavern in the Via dell'Abbondanza in Pompeii, with amphorae *stacked behind the bar.*

Below: Interior of a tavern at Ostia, 1st century AD. Most taverns were just for drinking but this one had a table and bench and may have served snacks or even full meals.

DINNER PARTIES

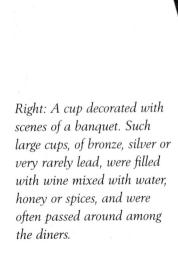

Above: A young servant girl, probably a slave, carrying a dish of food, from a fresco in the Villa of the Mysteries, Pompeii c. 60BC.

Towards evening, after their lengthy baths, Romans headed home for the meal that was usually the social highlight of the day: *cena*, dinner. This was eaten around the eighth hour in winter or ninth hour in summer, which is about 4–6 p.m. in modern terms, for the Roman day varied according to the season. Originally there had been three daily meals but by the late Republic the first two, *ientaculum* and *prandium*, seem to have become little more than snacks, eaten without formality or even a table. The *cena* was the great meal of the day, sometimes the occasion of excessive gourmandizing but more usually of modest meals, to which the Romans came bathed, in clean clothes if they had them.

THE DINING ROOM

All Romans who could afford it liked to dine reclining on *triclinia* (couches which ran on three sides of a table), set around a table, which gave the *triclinium* (dining room) its name. Covered with cushions and mattresses, these couches were sometimes built into the walls to save space. Others could be elaborately decorated and gilded. By the 2nd century BC women ate reclining alongside men. Only children and favoured slaves sat on stools or chairs at the end of the *triclinium*, a position which was considered undignified. Cato the Younger, one of Caesar's staunchest opponents, vowed never to eat reclining as long as Caesar's tyranny lasted, an extreme of self-denial more admired than imitated. (Cato committed suicide.) Some dining rooms were windowless, lit by oil lamps, but decorated with fine murals and mosaics. However, in country villas, *triclinia* could take advantage of the view seen through colonnades.

The couches were arranged around a table, one side of which was left free for service. The most honoured couch was opposite the empty side of the table and on each couch the most privileged position was that by the *fulcrum* or head of the couch. A *nomenclator* (usher) announced the guests and showed them their place on the couch, after they had removed their shoes. If more than nine people were to dine, other *triclinia* had to be brought in, twelve places being the usual maximum.

EATING AND DRINKING

M*instratores* (waiters) now brought in dishes and bowls. Diners had knives, toothpicks and several spoons, but as the Romans did not have forks, they ate mainly with their hands. They washed their hands frequently throughout the meal from bowls brought round by slaves. Every guest had his or her own napkin but some brought their own napkins with them which they filled with *apophoreta* (titbits) to take home. This was considered perfectly acceptable.

Right: A cup decorated with scenes of a banquet. Such large cups, of bronze, silver or very rarely lead, were filled with wine mixed with water, honey or spices, and were often passed around among the diners.

A grand *cena* could be formidable, an occasion for ostentatious display by the rich. Seven courses were not uncommon: a *gustatio* or hors d'oeuvre, three entrées, two roasts and a dessert. Juvenal *c.* AD120 described, "Huge lobsters garnished with asparagus…mullet from Corsica… goose's liver, a capon as big as a house, a piping hot boar…truffles and delicious mushrooms". Such descriptions might seem wildly exaggerated if not reiterated by the Greek historian Herodian 100 years later and by Macrobius, governor of Africa, in AD410. Juvenal also attacked hosts who kept the best dishes and wines for themselves and important guests, while giving "black meal" to the less important.

The Romans drank correspondingly. A first libation started the meal. *Mulsus* (honeyed wine) followed the first course and slaves went round refilling the *cratera* (mixing bowl), for wine was diluted with water. The proportion of water to wine could be low but generally it was somewhere in the region of 4:1.

After dinner there might be *acommissatio*, a drinking match in which diners had to empty their cups in one go. Dancers, clowns and striptease provided entertainment at some dinner parties, which could sometimes turn into orgies. Belching after such meals was perfectly acceptable and the emperor Claudius, who loved his food, considered an edict authorizing other emissions. But only the greediest diners vomited up their meal into pots held by slaves or on to the fine mosaic floors.

Only the length of such dinners tempered such excess, for they could go on for hours. Nero and his short-lived successor Vitellius, a noted gourmand, often stayed eating and drinking until after midnight, which was thought gross. Juvenal attacked those who "went to bed with the rise of Lucifer, the morning star, at an hour when our generals in the past would be moving their standards and camp".

Against such gourmandizing should be set the frugality of both Plinys. Pliny the Elder rose from the table when it was still light in summer and after only the first

hour of night in the winter, while his nephew praised "elegant but frugal meals". He accepted a dinner invitation once from Catilius Severus on the condition that "You treat me frugally and our table abounds only with philosophical conversation". Much more typical of most Roman meals than Neronian banquets was the dinner organized by the Funeral College in Rome for its members in AD133 at which each guest was given simply a loaf of bread, four sardines and an *amphora* of wine.

Above: A banquet in Carthage, depicted on a mosaic of the 4th century AD. *The diners appear to be sitting up, perhaps to view the performers.*

Below: This banquet scene from Ancona in eastern Italy shows the classic pattern of diners reclining on triclinia *arranged around three sides of a table, the fourth side being left free for servants.*

FOOD FOR RICH AND POOR

Above: Bread being sold at a bakery in Pompeii, a fresco of the 1st century AD. Note the flattened, circular shape of the baker's loaves.

Two things stand out about Roman attitudes towards food in general. The first is that they were almost omnivorous. "If it moves or grows, cook it and eat it" could have been their motto, for they lacked religious or sentimental dietary taboos (except against cannibalism, and they did not eat dogs or cats). A large type of dormouse was specially bred for eating and most song birds were considered fair game, or were bred in captivity. This catholic approach led to dishes of great variety and increasing complexity and richness on the tables of the rich in Rome and other great cities.

The other salient point is that meat was expensive and most people ate a simple diet, based on cereals, olive oil and vegetables with quite a lot of wine, and modest amounts of meat – principally pork, seldom beef or chicken – and seafood. Slaves and paupers ate often rancid cereals as a gruel or porridge and suffered chronic malnutrition, as modern analysis of skeletons at Pompeii has shown.

THE CHANGING DIET OF ROME

The early Roman diet was simple, based on cereals, olive oil and locally grown vegetables. Later orators used to praise the ancient frugality of Curius Dentatus, who "gathered his scanty vegetables and cooked them himself in his little stove". This moderation did not long survive Rome's rise to wealth and power.

From 200BC on, Rome could no longer be supplied locally and soon foreign wars led to imports of entirely new foods. Lucullus, the great late Republican general, for example, introduced the cherry to Rome from Asia Minor. However, most of the bulk of the food sucked into Rome remained the essential supplies of wheat, which came from Egypt, Africa and Sicily, and olive oil which came from Africa and Spain.

There were many other dishes but, as the Romans had no refrigeration, most perishable foods tended to be produced and eaten locally. Martial's *Epigrams* list

Right: From 200BC on, Rome began to import food, metals, textiles and other goods from a growing range of countries around the Mediterranean both for their luxuries and as staple necessities.

the many foods available for those who could afford them at the end of the 1st century AD. Pork came from Gaul, cured meats from Spain, spices from Asia, wines and fruits – including apples, pears, figs, grapes, melons and plums – from vineyards and orchards in Italy, along with asparagus (a favourite of Augustus), olives, beans, lentils, radishes, peas, pumpkins, lettuce and cabbages.

Seafood in all its variety was much prized in an empire centred on the sea. Red mullet and shellfish, especially lobster, were delicacies, but oysters were not a luxury and were transported inland along the roads, even in Britain, to be eaten by travellers. From the edges of the Sahara in Africa came pomegranates and dates, and fresh game came from the woods of Italy. Most dishes were cooked in sauces flavoured with spices from the East such as pepper. Perhaps the most characteristic Roman flavouring was *garum*. This was made from fish guts, salted and placed in tanks in the sun until they had gained sufficient potency to be used to flavour dishes – a process that could take four to six weeks.

By the 1st century AD Roman cuisine in all its sometimes overwhelming intricacy is revealed – albeit in caricatured form – in the great banquet that Trimalchio gave in the *Satyricon*, where the chef could create "'a fish out of a sow's belly, a wood pigeon out of bacon, a turtledove out of ham". Dormice "sprinkled with honey and poppy seed" made an amazing hors d'oeuvre and a boar stuffed with live thrushes that flew out as it was being carved made an eye-catching main roast. Although such absurdly complex courses must have been rare, Roman cooks delighted in concocting dishes that were unusual. However, as the still-life murals of bread, fruit and game from Pompeii suggest, most families would normally have eaten far more simply. Sausages, meat pies and cubes of roasted meat were popular, along with fruits both fresh and dried and buns filled with both savoury and sweet things. Honey was the universal sweetener.

WHAT THE ROMANS LACKED

Ancient Romans did not have citrus fruits such as oranges or grapefruit, nor rice, sugar, apricots, coffee, pheasant or peaches, all of which were introduced by the Arabs to Europe during the Middle Ages. They did not have tomatoes, potatoes, corn, peanuts, guinea fowl, red and green (bell) peppers, chocolate and turkey, which came to Europe from Central or North America in the 16th century.

The Romans did not drink tea, which was still a Chinese secret, and they scarcely ate butter, for it apparently seldom occurred to them to store surplus milk in this way. In fact, they did not eat much in the way of dairy products apart from cheese. Their diet approximated to the modern ideal of the Mediterranean diet.

Above: A still life showing fruit, nuts and a water jug from the House of the Stags at Herculaneum, 1st century AD. This fresco illustrates what the well-to-do Roman mainly ate better than some more elaborate written menus.

Below: Seafood of many types was much-prized by the Romans, both rich and also the poor if they lived near the sea. Lobster and mullet were thought delicacies. The Mediterranean in those unpolluted days still teemed with abundant marine life.

WINE AND VINEYARDS

Above: The Romans had over 50 distinct varieties of grapes, but most of their wine was red.

Wine played a hugely important role in Roman life, for they had no tea, chocolate or coffee, nor soft drinks nor spirits. They hardly drank beer from the middle Republic on – they knew of it but considered it fit mainly for Germans, although beer was drunk by Roman soldiers on Hadrian's Wall. Romans drank wine, an estimated 100 million litres a year in Rome alone at its peak, most of which came from outside central Italy. For the undernourished majority, wine was an important food, a source of minerals, vitamins (including, we now know, vital anti-oxidants) and sugars. Slaves drank water with a little thin wine.

ROMAN VITICULTURE

The Greeks had long grown wine in southern Italy, from where viticulture spread north to central Italy. Etruria was thought to produce some of Rome's best wines, such as Graviscanum, Caeres or Tiburtinum, but the especially renowned Falernian wine came from just north of Naples. Most famous vineyards were not far from the coast, as sea transport was so much cheaper than land transport. Greek wine was also highly regarded by the Romans, although it may not have tasted like Greek wines today. Spain later became another major wine exporter. Wine transported long distances in pinewood barrels may have acquired a resinous tang like modern retsina, but the Romans do not seem to have objected as they added various flavourings to their wine when they mixed them.

As trade around the empire boomed in the three centuries after 100BC, wine-growing spread to new regions. The Greek cities of southern Gaul, especially Marseilles, had always grown wine and under the Romans viticulture reached northern Gaul. In AD71 Pliny the Elder noted that vineyards already existed around Bordeaux but he knew little about their wines and they remained obscure. The warmer and drier Rhône valley was more promising territory for a viticulture based on Mediterranean methods and grape varieties. Trier, surrounded by sun-trapping vineyards hanging from the steep slopes above the river Moselle, may have produced wine as early as the 2nd century AD. However, evidence of its flourishing vineyards comes only from the second half of the 4th century AD, in a

Left: Pressing grapes in a winery from St Romain en Gal, France, c. AD200. Vine-growing was introduced into southern France by the Greeks.

famous poem by the imperial tutor, governor and poet Ausonius, supported by archaeological evidence in the form of wine presses in the Moselle valley at Piesport. The Moselle flowing past Trier, the Western empire's capital at the time, reminded Ausonius of his native Bordeaux, where vineyards lined the river Garonne. He described wealthy villas with their smoking chimneys, boatmen exchanging jocular insults with men working among the vines, fish playing in the river and, in a famous passage, the hills mirrored in the Moselle's waters.

What colour paints the river shallows, when Hesperus has brought the shades of evening.
The Moselle is dyed with the green of her hills; their tops quiver
In the ripples, vine leaves tremble from afar
And the grape clusters swell even in the clear stream.

The most informative Roman author on viticultural matters was Lucius Junius Columella in the 1st century AD. In *De re Rustica* (*About Rural Matters*) he wrote about many aspects of farming beside vineyards, but he did discuss different grape varieties and how to balance quantity against quality. He listed more than 50 grape varieties and praised a native Italian variety called the Amminean.

The Romans sometimes used to trail vines along elms and other trees such as poplars for support, and it has been suggested that the traditional English elm (now almost extinct) was first imported into Britain by Romans for such purposes.

Bacchus, the wine god, was an important deity to the Romans and libations, the pouring out of wine in honour of a god, were a common sacramental use of wine. The last of a particularly good wine was sometimes thrown on the floor

Right: Although the Romans drank wine regularly, being seen drunk in public as in this Hellenistic statue of an old woman was considered a disgraceful condition and was not the norm.

as an offering to the gods. Later, as the empire slowly became Christian, the frequent use of wine in the Eucharist again encouraged the spread of viticulture into northern Europe, for wine remained expensive to transport long distances until Bordeaux began shipping its wines north in the 12th century.

VINTAGES AND WINE STORAGE

Although the Romans may not have had completely airtight corks (they used lead as an extra sealant) they did develop glass bottles besides traditional pottery *amphorae* for better wines. These were marked with a distinguishing *pittacium* (label) stating their vintage. The Romans apparently kept certain of their finest wines for a remarkably long time. Horace when middle-aged wrote of drinking a vintage older than himself, and the most famous vintage, that dating from the consulate of Opimius in 121BC, was reputedly kept for 125 years. However, most Roman wines were drunk young when they were sharp, even rough, and strong. The Romans never drank their wine neat, but diluted it with water, sometimes with seawater, or they sweetened the wine with honey. Roman wines at times might have tasted like sangria.

Above: Late 2nd-century AD bottle and drinking glass from the mosaic pavement of a triclinium (dining room) at Thysdrus, El Djem.

ROME THE GREAT CONSUMER

Above: The symbols of grain merchants in a mosaic set in the street leading to the market in Ostia, Rome's great harbour town, c. AD100.

Below: Amphorae (earthenware jars) for transporting and storing oil and wine came in a variety of shapes and sizes, but under the empire their shapes were increasingly standardized. These amphorae come from a sunken ship.

One of the chief concerns of those governing Rome, from the later Republic until the end of the ancient city in the 6th century AD, was supplying it with essential foods. Other large cities imported grain, but Rome's demands eclipsed all others.

WHEAT, WINE AND OIL
Since Clodius started the free distribution to male citizens over the age of ten of five *modii* per month of grain (880lbs/400kg per person of grain annually) in 58BC, rulers who failed to provide the *annona* (dole) faced riots. The emperor Claudius (AD41–54) was pelted with stale crusts by a hungry crowd after a poor harvest and storms delayed the grain fleets.

Claudius' response was to build a giant artificial harbour north of Ostia at Portus, which Trajan improved with an inland basin 60 years later. Grain, mainly wheat, and olive oil were the staples of the Roman diet, but olive oil also lit the city's countless oil lamps and was lavishly used for personal hygiene, in place of soap. Wine was almost the only drink available.

Wheat, wine and oil were therefore needed in unprecedented quantities – about 400,000 tons per year of foodstuffs, of which 240,000 tons were wheat. (Meat, seafood, fruit and vegetables, supplementary to these dietary basics, are less easily estimated, although early in the 3rd century AD Septimius Severus added oil, and in AD275 Aurelian pork and wine, to the *annona*, but by then the city's population was beginning to fall.)

The great mound rising beside the Tiber in Rome known as Monte Testaccio is made of pieces of broken *amphorae* (earthenware jars). Rising 112ft (34m), it has a circumference of 3,200ft (1km) and contains fragments of at least 53 million *amphorae*. The majority once held olive oil shipped from Spain in the years AD140–250. Africa was another large source of oil. Most *amphorae* came in a variety of standardized sizes. They were designed to be neatly stacked in ships' holds. They were usually broken up after being emptied because their interiors absorbed oil which went rancid, although a few were later used to lighten architectural vaults.

About 1,000 shiploads of wheat were needed for Rome each year, as the average merchant ship carried about 240 tons. Inclusion of the shipping needed for the estimated 100 million litres (22 million gallons) of wine and 20 million litres (4 million gallons) of oil would boost this total to at least 1,700 ships a year arriving at Rome's ports – excluding those lost.

Most ships arrived in the sailing season, which lasted 100–120 days a year. The Romans never developed state-controlled fleets but relied on private contractors, whom they encouraged in various ways. After the bread riots Claudius offered anyone who used a ship holding at least 10,000 *modii* (70 tons) to supply Rome, privileges ranging from citizenship for non-citizens to exemptions from various taxes.

Emperors from Augustus on appointed officials such as the *praefectus annonae* (wheat dole prefect), who soon acquired assistants. By AD200, the *sub-praefectus annonae* (wheat dole subprefect), was paid 100,000 sesterces, a large salary reflecting his importance. However, grain supplies always remained precariously dependent on the caprices of harvests and of storms at sea. A serious grain shortage in AD190 caused riots which the emperor Commodus only defused by having Cleander, his favourite minister, executed as a scapegoat.

HAULAGE AND STORAGE

When the food reached Rome's ports of Pozzuoli, Ostia or Portus it had to be unloaded, dragged up the river and stored. Grain and oil had to be rowed or hauled the 20 miles (32km) up the Tiber from the port in smaller boats or barges in a journey that took two to three days.

Four types of boat were used: the *scaphae*, *lintres* and *lenunculi*, all rowing boats, and the *codicariae*, specialized boats used to transport goods from Ostia and Portus up river to Rome. These had oars and lowerable masts but were often rowed or hauled, less often by slaves than by free but poor casual labourers. Although they had to be hauled upstream, they could be rowed or sailed downstream. The Romans did not use horses for haulage, as they never developed suitable horse collars. The boat haulers, known as *helciarii*, used to chant rhythmically as they trudged along pulling their heavy vessels up stream towards the city. They even had their own guild. Upon arrival in Rome, the grain, oil and wine were stored in *horrea*, specially built warehouses by the Tiber such as those below the Aventine Hill in the region called Marmorata (so-called because this is where the marble coming into Rome was unloaded).

Some *horrea* were immense: the Horrea Galbana, for example, had 140 rooms on the ground floor alone and covered about 5 acres (2ha). These multistorey warehouses were massively built, with walls at least 2ft (60cm) thick. They had small external windows and massive doors to preserve their valuable contents from thieves. Inside they had large internal windows, both between rooms and opening on to courtyards, to provide plentiful ventilation to keep the grain dry. For the same reason they normally had raised floors. The floors also stopped rodent activity and provided circulation of air to prevent the spontaneous combustion of overheated grain. Much grain was lost to rodents nonetheless.

Above: Men, either free labourers or slaves, hauling a barge full of wine barrels up a river, probably the Rhône, since the relief comes from Avignon. The Romans could not use horses for such work as they did not have the right type of horsecollar.

Below: Many warehouses were monumental structures boasting fine architectural features, such as this grand gateway of the Horrea Epagathania in Ostia, whose pediment and pillars are worthy of a public building.

TUNICS AND TOGAS

Below: This Roman magistrate from Asia Minor in the 5th century AD wears similar clothes to those worn 500 years before.

It is striking how little fashions changed from the late Republic to the end of the Western empire 600 years later. A senator from Cicero's day might have looked rather oddly dressed four centuries later but he would not have seemed to be wearing fancy dress. The same could not be said today. The very slowly changing nature of Roman fashion, however, is more typical of most societies around the world than the increasingly rapid sartorial changes of recent centuries. Clothes generally denoted status in the Roman world and, while definitions of social status changed gradually, fashions were never dictated by designers, nor did individuals dress solely according to their own whims. Although the odd dandy like Caesar wore his toga with particularly wide sleeves, the Romans were generally rather puritanical about what citizens should wear, adhering to a simplicity that can be called classical.

TYPES OF FABRIC

The basic Roman garment for all classes was the *tunicum*, a simple tunic made of wool or, less commonly, linen. Cotton was rare for a long time and silk was always a luxury item imported from furthest Asia. Although the use of silk increased steadily, for a long time it was thought utterly effeminate for men. (Caligula caused a scandal by appearing once in gaudy silk robes.) However, under the Principate it became increasingly common for richer women. Finally, in the grandiose courts of the later empire (after AD284) most courtiers wore elaborate silk robes. Wool, undyed for

Above: A Roman wearing a pallium *(cloak) over his tunic from Sicily, 4th century AD. Only richer citizens could afford a* pallium.

poor people and white for richer citizens, remained the commonest material, however. The *tunicum* was made of two pieces of cloth sewn together, usually untailored so that the surplus produced short sleeves, with a belt around the waist. Slaves, labourers and the very poor wore almost nothing else, but richer citizens often wore a *pallium* or Greek-style cloak over their longer *tunicum*. It is possible that some Romans wore a *licium*, a loin cloth, as underwear.

Formal dress for male Roman citizens consisted of the toga, a large semicircular piece of woollen cloth about 9ft (2.7m) long worn draped over one shoulder to leave the other bare and almost reaching the ankles. Exactly how this was put on has been tentatively reconstructed. A toga was certainly a cumbersome, heavy garment, which citizens liked to discard as soon as possible but which emperors repeatedly tried to make citizens wear in public as late as the reign of Commodus

(AD180–92). In the evenings a *synthesis*, a comfortable compromise between a toga and a tunic, was often worn for dining on a couch. Senators were distinguished from ordinary citizens by the *laticlava*, a broad purple stripe running down their tunics, while equestrians had a narrower stripe, the *angusticlava*. Emperors wore the most purple, so "being raised to the purple" came to mean becoming emperor.

Hooded cloaks, *paenulae*, could be worn over the tunic or toga in bad weather but hats were generally unknown apart from straw hats worn informally against the sun. In bad weather part of the toga could be pulled over the head for protection, as it was for priestly roles. Trousers were known to the Romans but were long considered barbarous garments – worn by Persians and Germans – and were only adopted partially at the end of the empire, in a sign for conservatives of general decay. Clerical dress in the Catholic and Episcopalian or Lutheran churches, with its long, superimposed robes, still perpetuates old Roman dress. In the later empire, heavy military-style belts were worn by bureaucrats as well as soldiers, revealing the general militarization of Roman government.

WOMEN'S WEAR

Roman women also wore long loose tunics. These, called *stolae*, were often in bright colours and of fine material, such as good linen, cotton or silk. Underneath they often wore a *strophium*, a leather band that served as a simple bra. Over their *stola* went a rectangular woollen mantle, the *palla*, which was draped over the left shoulder, across the back and under the right arm. Prostitutes and convicted adulteresses wore female togas, the former often wearing transparent silks.

Women's dress also seems to have changed remarkably little over the centuries, although brooches – buttons were unknown to the Romans – became progressively more elaborate, as did jewellery generally.

FOOTWEAR

The basic Roman footwear was the sandal in varying shapes. The *solea* was a form of basic sandal of a type still worn by some Catholic monks, with the sole attached to the instep by straps. *Crepidae* were sandals secured by a strap passing through eyelets, while *calcei* were leather half boots with crossed laces. In the army soldiers wore *caligae*, hobnailed boots that laced up round the ankle. (*Caligula*, Little Boots, was the nickname of the emperor Gaius, who grew up in the camp of his father Germanicus.) The Romans increasingly wore *fasciae*, a form of puttee, around the feet and lower legs, in northern parts of the empire and in winter. Women wore either sandals or soft leather shoes, but high heels were unknown. Socks were sometimes worn.

Above: As these women conversing on a mural from Pompeii c. AD70 show, Roman women wore long, loose brightly-coloured stolae (tunics) of linen, cotton or silk. Their fashions changed only very slowly over the centuries.

Right: A pair of leather sandals from Egypt of the 3rd century AD. Sandals were the standard footwear across areas around the Mediterranean.

HAIRSTYLES AND COSMETICS

Above: The curly beard and hair of the 2nd century AD as sported by Lucius Verus.

Below: Women's hairstyles became very elaborate, then reverted to simpler styles with hair tied back and a middle parting, as in this Egyptian mummy portrait of the 4th century AD.

Although Roman clothing changed very slowly, hairstyles and fashions in beards underwent remarkable developments that perhaps reveal something about wider changes in Roman society itself.

BEARDED OR CLEAN-SHAVEN?
In the early Republic, according to tradition – such as the story about the Gauls pulling at the beards of elderly senators during the sack of Rome in 390BC – and in surviving portraits such as the so-called "Brutus", men had beards and short hair. The Romans always remained short-haired but by *c.* 150BC most Roman men were clean-shaven, possibly following Hellenistic styles. Fashion dictated that they remained so until after the death of Trajan in AD117. (A few soldiers had earlier had clipped beards and moustaches.)

Shaving was not, however, an easy or pain-free task for Romans, as they lacked both soap (for working up a lather) and high-quality steel for a clean shave. It was difficult and unusual even to try to shave oneself. Important Romans used to have barbers come to shave them in their houses and some, like Augustus, carried on their daily business at the same time. Ordinary Romans visited regularly but not always daily the *tonsor* (barber).

The barber's shop, the *tonstrina*, opened on to the street and was the place where men came to exchange news and gossip. Here they had their hair cut and their faces shaved, by a *novacula*, a blunt iron razor, by a form of poultice called *dropax*, made of several types of wax that depilated rather than shaved, or by *forcipes aduncae*, tweezers. The whole process was long and painful. Skilled barbers could make a lot of money; the unskilled made a painful mess of their customers' faces.

When Hadrian, either because he had a scar on his face that he wished to hide or because of his love of all things Greek, began wearing a beard after AD117, the fashion quickly spread and soon almost all Roman men sported beards. In the 4th century AD fashion changed again. Constantine always appears in his portraits clean-shaven, as do his sons. Julian, in emotive reaction against his Christian precursors, wore a beard like a Greek philosopher. Although Julian's successors were mostly clean-shaven, by the 6th century AD most men were bearded again.

While beards came and went, male hairstyles – with the flamboyant exception of Nero and some of his courtiers, who adopted *bouffant* big hair copying that of charioteers – remained short and generally plain until the 2nd century AD. They then became steadily more elaborate. Hadrian is shown with a head of curly hair and soon men adopted hairdos of really elaborate complexity. Lucius Verus, the idle co-emperor of Marcus Aurelius, had a tremendous head of curly hair, but so had the ascetic Marcus and the militaristic Septimius Severus, emperors who followed rather than set the style. Their intricate curls reflect the barbers' skills. The latter used combs or a *calamistrum*, a heated curling iron, and even dyed some customers' hair. In the catastrophe-ridden 3rd century AD, men's hair became short and plain again, as Gallienus' and Diocletian's respectively austere and grim busts attest.

WOMEN'S COIFFURE

Hairstyles for women in the Republic were simple, with the hair drawn back from a central parting and gathered in a chignon at the nape of the neck. Under Augustus, women's hair was often braided and with Messalina, Claudius' notoriously unfaithful wife, high-piled hairstyles appeared. Under the Flavian emperors and Trajan (AD69–117) female hair became extremely complicated, with great masses of curls piled high on the head. Trajan's sister Marciana and his niece Matilda both dressed their hair in diadems, "high as towers", the product of long hours spent with their *ornatrix*, or hairdresser.

Imperious Roman women of the nobility were prone to lash out at any hairdresser who failed to please them – many were slaves – at least according to the poet Martial, who tells of "Lalage avenging with the mirror in which she had seen it [an unfortunate hairdo] and Plecusa falls, hit because of those unruly locks of hair". Juvenal mocked women whose "numerous tiers and storeys piled upon one another on the head" made them look taller than they really were. Later hairstyles were less elaborate. Wigs were occasionally used to disguise baldness.

COSMETICS

In addition to her work as a hairdresser, an *ornatrix* also took care of wealthier women's makeup. Often lead-based – the Romans were not aware of the dangers of

lead – the cosmetics were stored in glass phials or flagons and alabaster vases. Creams, perfumes and unguents were extensively used. Red for the lips and cheeks was made from ochre, a lichen-like plant called *ficus* or from molluscs. Eyeliner was made from soot or powders of antimony, which was also used to thicken the eyebrows. Mirrors, an essential part of the daily toilette, were made of highly polished metal, for true mirrors of reflecting glass were unknown. Ovid, ever aware of the erotic side of life, advised women to bolt the door of their chamber when making themselves up for "[your beauty] lies stored in a hundred caskets". Women also adorned themselves with elaborate jewellery, including *armillae* (bracelets), *catellae* (trinkets) and *periscelides* (ankle circlets).

Above: A woman pouring perfume into a flask from the Villa Farnesina, c. AD10.

Below: A casket containing a wealthy Roman woman's toilette items from Cumae.

EROTIC LOVE

Above: Tombstone showing a brothel-keeper and customer. Prostitution was accepted and regulated in Rome.

Below: An erotic fresco from Pompeii. Many Romans enjoyed often fine erotic art such as this in private.

The Roman reputation for widespread sexual debauchery is hardly merited. It derives more from Suetonius' racy portraits of the first 12 Caesars, reinforced by Hollywood films and discoveries of "shocking" pictures at Pompeii, than from the reality of life for most people in the Roman world, who seldom had the opportunity for sexual depravity. Most of them worked hard, married young and remained reasonably faithful. If there were no lethal sexually transmitted diseases to discourage promiscuity, there were no contraceptives to facilitate it either. Prostitution existed, was recognized but not revered (unlike in Babylon or parts of Syria), and was regulated. Prostitutes wore distinctive toga-style dresses.

However, if unworried by Christian fears of eternal damnation for extramarital sex, the Romans were very concerned with the maintenance of public dignity and social stability, both of which were based on the conventional family unit. Monogamy within marriage was always the ideal and female "virtue" (chastity) was much praised in the legends of early Rome. Lucretia, a noble Roman virgin killed herself rather than give in to the advances of the Etruscan tyrant Tarquinius. (Tarquinius was soon after expelled from Rome.) However, as with most pagan religions, minor fertility gods around the empire were honoured by sometimes ithyphallic statues, while statues of major deities, often half-naked, adorned public places. These can give ancient cities an unwarranted air of eroticism to modern eyes.

SEXUAL MORALITY

Heterosexual romance and love were the main themes of many novels, plays and poetry, from the numerous plays of Plautus in the 2nd century BC to Longus' romantic novel *Daphnis and Chloe* 300 years later. Here the naivity of the peasant lovers is mocked. Apuleius, writing *The Golden Ass* at about the same time, caters to a more sophisticated audience, but he attributes bad faith and perversity to characters with Greek names.

In the late Republic there had been a marked loosening of sexual restrictions, at least among upper class Romans. Augustus tried to control this. The *Lex Julia* made adultery a criminal offence and he banished his own daughter, grand-daughter and the poet Ovid for sexual immorality. Augustus himself, however, had mistresses. Women, making use of their new freedoms, could choose or reject lovers, but women's own voices are seldom heard. That of Messalina, Claudius' notoriously promiscuous wife, is exceptional. Lesbianism presumably existed but escaped record because writers were men.

HOMOSEXUALITY

The Romans had no specific word for male homosexuality, for they seldom thought in terms of predetermined sexual orientation but rather about public behaviour. While the Romans never idealized homosexuality as some upper-class Greeks had, they did not demonize it either, as Christians later did. Homosexuality was, however, often considered a Greek habit and, as with most things Greek, it seems to have become more widespread in the later Republic. Augustus typically tried to discourage it by legislation in his attempt to boost the birth rate among citizens. Petronius' *Satyricon* involved the adventures of characters – bisexuals of singular cynicism – with Greek names in the still Greek cities of southern Italy. However, Roman poets such as Tibullus and Horace also revealed homosexual sentiments.

There remained a strong sexist bias in Roman attitudes to homosexuality: men who took the passive or female role in such relations were despised and risked losing their citizenship – hence the force of stories circulated by his political enemies that Julius Caesar, when young, had been King Nicomedes of Bithynia's boyfriend. (Caesar later became a noted womanizer.) Emperors like Nero who allowed themselves to be penetrated – according to Suetonius Nero appeared dressed as the bride at his own mock-wedding – forfeited public respect. Public decorum was the key.

When the popular Titus became emperor in AD79, he put aside his harem of catamites along with his much-loved Jewish mistress the princess Berenice. (The latter was thought unacceptable because she was an exotic royal foreigner rather than because of any Roman anti-semitism.) Trajan took a harem of boys with him on campaign but, as he was even more popular than Titus, this was accepted, at least outside Rome. By contrast, Hadrian's prolonged mourning for his boyfriend Antinous, who drowned in the Nile, struck many as excessive and undignified for an emperor. Emperors such as Caligula in the 1st century AD and Elagabalus in the 3rd century AD behaved so outrageously in public – Elagabalus reputedly prostituted himself – that they were soon assassinated.

From the 3rd century AD on, attitudes towards sex began to change. If Christians were the only real ascetics – Origen castrated himself to avoid the temptations of a beautiful young female pupil – non-Christians too began to become more obviously restrained in their behaviour. Herodian's novel *The Ethiopian Story* of the 3rd century AD praises the fidelity of its two engaged young lovers so strongly that Christians later claimed him as a covert co-religionist, which he probably was not. However Neoplatonism, the dominant philosophy in the later empire, tended to regard the flesh as something to be transcended, an attitude dating back to Plato which now became increasingly common. On this point at least pagan and Christian could meet.

Above: An erotic scene from a bedroom in the huge villa at Piazza Armerina, Sicily, c. AD320, shows that Roman enjoyment of carnal pleasure persisted into the later empire.

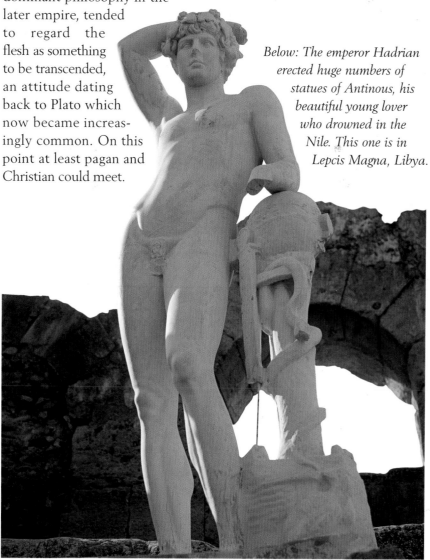

Below: The emperor Hadrian erected huge numbers of statues of Antinous, his beautiful young lover who drowned in the Nile. This one is in Lepcis Magna, Libya.

FUNERALS AND THE AFTERLIFE

Above: The Mausoleum of Augustus in Rome, completed 28BC, housed the funerary urns of members of the imperial family and was once topped by cypress trees, a custom going back to the Etruscans.

Below: A women's funerary choir performing a ritual dance from a tomb in Ruvo of the 5th century BC. Greek beliefs and customs deeply influenced Rome's in this field as in many others.

The pagan Romans never had a consistent or united view about what happened to them after death. Beliefs varied greatly, from the uncompromising materialism of Lucretius, the poetic adherent of Epicurus who believed that we simply become again our constituent atoms, to the far more common belief that some aspect of an individual might survive death, but probably not in a very agreeable way. Only with the Roman world's gradual conversion to Christianity in the 4th and 5th centuries AD did fixed beliefs in heaven and hell emerge.

THE ROMAN AFTERLIFE

Before then, people generally took what seemed most attractive – or least incredible – from what has been called the "inherited conglomerate" of myths, legends and beliefs that was constantly added to over the centuries but never reformed or subtracted from. The original Roman mixture of Etruscan and Greek ideas, in which the first was initially the most significant, was later enriched by new religions such as the cults of Bacchus, Isis and Mithras, which promised their adherents salvation. There were as well as the secretive, mystical sects such as the Pythagoreans and Orphics, who apparently believed in metempsychosis (reincarnation as animals or even plants).

For most people in the Roman world, however, the afterlife was a gloomy place of shadows and sometimes of torment, hardly more cheerful than the Christian or Muslim ideas of hell, which they may well have influenced. (The early Jews had had little belief in life after death.) In Book VI of Virgil's *The Aeneid*, which soon became Rome's national epic, Aeneas visits Hades, the underworld, and there talks to the shade of his father Anchises, for he was a notably filial son. This is an obvious reference to Odysseus' not dissimilar experience in Homer's *Odyssey*, and apposite as Roman ideas of the underworld were influenced by the Greeks. However, the Roman view of Hades was perhaps even gloomier, following Etruscan beliefs.

According to the composite Graeco-Roman story, Hades, the shadowy underworld, was governed by Pluto, sometimes called Orcus, the god of wealth as well as death. The souls of the dead were carried off by *genii*, spirits, who could be good or evil. This kingdom had several entrances through caves on Earth, but to reach it the dead had to pass Cerberus, the many-headed hound who guarded its gates. They then crossed the River Styx by paying Charon, the boatman, an obol, who became identified with Charun, a sinister Etruscan god of the dead. Sometimes Rhadamynthus and Minos, legendary kings of Crete, would then judge the souls of the dead, most of whom were left in a fearful limbo. Only a few heroes or deified emperors were thought to escape to the Elysian fields. Another infernal deity was Dis Pater, whom the Romans feared and seldom worshipped openly.

Such dismal views of the afterworld frightened many ordinary people. Writers like Lucretius, Cicero and Seneca, all infused with different aspects of Greek

Left: These Roman tombs in the Isola Sacra cemetery near Ostia, probably dating from the 2nd century AD, would have housed many members of the same family over the years. By then burial was becoming common.

philosophy, tried in vain to reassure them. However, most Romans regarded life on Earth as the important thing, not as a mere trial before eternal life in heaven, as Christians were meant to do.

TOMB TYPES

One of the laws of the famous Twelve Tables of 451BC forbade burial within the sacred *pomerium* (city boundary) so, as Rome grew, burial sites were pushed outward by the expansion of the city. Tombs and burials were traditionally located along the roads out of the city, at least for the wealthy, from the Forum Romanum and the Esquiline Hill to the Campus Martius, an early favourite location between the Servian Wall and the Tiber. Here Augustus built a mausoleum for his own family, but this area too was rapidly built over. Soon cemeteries began to line the roads leading out of Rome, especially the Via Appia to the south, where many fine tombs still stand.

Augustus' Mausoleum, started in 28BC, is typical in revealing marked Etruscan influences although the Greeks and Persians had also had *tumuli*: circular masonry drums topped by conical earth mounds, on which trees were often planted. Hadrian's great mausoleum across the Tiber, built *c.* AD135 to house

his own and the Antonine dynasty's remains, now the Castel Sant'Angelo, perpetuates something of the same tradition but with stronger Greek influences. An alternative type of tomb, probably derived from Hellenistic Syria, consisted of several superimposed columnar structures with either a pyramidal or a conical roof. Diocletian built an octagonal mausoleum for his body in his retirement palace at Split, while his successor Galerius erected an equally grand monument to himself. Built at Thessalonica a few years later in *c.* AD311, it is now a church.

Below: Funeral relief of a woman from Rome, dating from the 2nd century AD but with a Greek inscription, indicating that the woman was Greek in origin and thereby demonstrating the cosmopolitan nature of Rome's population.

Above: Funerary banqueting scene on the urn of Julia Eleutherides (a Greek surname but Roman first name), from the 2nd century AD.

Below: Funerary relief showing mourners bearing the catafalque of a body in procession from Rome, 1st century AD. A banquet normally followed the cremation or burial.

One of the most eye-catching of all tombs in Rome and still almost intact, is the "Pyramid of Cestius". Erected south of the city *c.* 20BC, near the later Porta Ostiensis and housing the remains of an important Roman noble, it recalls in its form the brief passion for Egyptiana that followed the annexation of that kingdom to the empire in 30BC. However, few later nobles outside the imperial family built on such a large scale. Probably the most unusual imperial tomb is Trajan's. The ashes of this popular emperor, who died in Tarsus in AD117 after the failure of his Parthian campaign, were placed inside his great column in the heart of Rome. A special senatorial decree overrode the ancient laws to permit the interment.

OTHER TOMBS

Not all tombs were grandiose dynastic statements, for many ordinary inhabitants both of the capital and other cities wanted to perpetuate their names, partly as a protest against the anonymity of metropolitan life, partly because, with such doubts about immortality, they wanted to be remembered after their deaths. Both interiors and exteriors were richly decorated, to impress the living and provide a fitting *domus aeterna* (eternal home) for the dead. The Romans often buried grave goods to accompany the dead, with elaborate furnishings suggesting an almost Egyptian belief in the deceased's continued existence. A fine example of such decorations comes from the painted stucco vaulting of the Mausoleum of the Anicii of the 2nd century AD.

A flamboyant but non-aristocratic tomb has been preserved at the Porta Maggiore in the Aurelianic Wall. This is the Tomb of Eurysaces, a wealthy baker and freedman of the late 1st century BC. The circular openings in the tomb probably emulate baker's ovens. The tomb of the Haterii, a family of rich builders, is another fine example of a resplendent non-aristocratic tomb.

Poorer citizens might subscribe to a burial club that would arrange a decent funeral for them, while all but the very poorest had their graves marked by *amphorae* buried in the ground up to their necks. Many survive in the Isola Sacra cemetery near Ostia. The inscriptions on some tombs can be humorous: "Here in my tomb I drain my cup more greedily, because here I must sleep and here must stay for ever". However, more often they are simply poignant: "May the passer-by who has seen these flowers and read this epitaph say to himself: 'This flower is Flavia's body'".

FUNERAL RITES

A funeral began with the laying out of the corpse for seven days so that friends and relatives could pay their last respects. There followed a funeral procession to the burial place where there was usually a funerary banquet, like a wake. The family would return regularly to the tomb during their mourning period, the first time only eight days later. They would continue to have commemorative picnics for long after. If the funeral was that of an important person, the procession might wend its way to the Forum Romanum, where a funeral oration would be given. Originally these were reserved for men only, but by the 1st century AD exceptional women were also honoured in this way. Occasionally, as with the speech Mark Antony gave at Caesar's funeral, such speeches had political significance.

Cremation on a pyre in public was the usual form of disposing of bodies for most Romans up to *c.* AD100, when fashions began to change for reasons that are not entirely clear. The change seems to have begun among the upper classes – although the emperors themselves long continued the custom of cremation – and then spread down through the social hierarchy. Whether this can be connected with the slow changes in other attitudes is unknown. It certainly encouraged some splendid sarcophagi, but the mythological scenes carved on them seldom suggest any very powerful belief in an afterlife. Typical scenes show cavorting Tritons and Nereids, mermen and sea nymphs, as on a sarcophagus in the Louvre. Battle scenes were also very popular, usually showing the sack of Troy or some other well-known legend, but few suggest any specific religious belief.

Christian attitudes towards tombs and burial were very different. As they confidently expected the resurrection of the body, cremation was always out of the question. Bodies were buried, sometimes in Rome's catacombs by both pagans and Christians, especially the latter, for Christians often wanted to keep a low profile even when not trying to avoid persecution. There the Greek word for fish, *ichthys*, served as an acrostic for the words "Jesus Christ, God's Son [and] Saviour". When Constantine made Christianity the imperially favoured cult, Christian art and iconography developed. The finest surviving early such tomb is the Mausoleum of Santa Constanza, a circular building whose interior is graced by delightful paintings of birds and flowers with no obvious religious connotations.

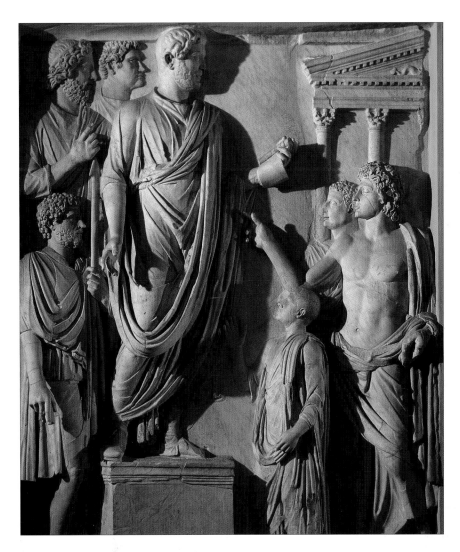

THE CULT OF THE ANCESTORS

Despite being in the underworld, the dead were strongly believed to haunt the living and therefore needed to be appeased – hence the origins of the gladiatorial games and their name *munera* (offerings). As the Christian writer Tertullian scathingly noted in *The Shows c.* AD200, "Men believed that the souls of the dead were propitiated by human blood". (Tertullian also disapproved of those tombs that invited the passing to drink to the deceased's memory.) *Mos maiorum*, the customs of our ancestors, always had a strong appeal to the Romans as an ideal, for Roman piety and dynastic pride were both connected with honouring the dead. The family death masks were kept prominently in the *domus*, normally in the atrium, and taken out and paraded through the streets on special occasions.

Above: Hadrian giving the funeral oration of his wife Sabina in the Forum Romanum, 2nd century AD.

Below: Vault of Santa Constanza, Rome, the Mausoleum of Constantine's daughter Constantia.

WITHDRAWN

INDEX